2Steps2Happiness:
It's Closer Than You Think

Your Guidebook To Greater Happiness

by

Dr. Adam M. Epstein

Dr. Adam M. Epstein is a Personal Life Coach who resides in Palm Beach County, Florida. He has a Doctor of Psychology (Psy.D.) Degree in Clinical Psychology from Nova Southeastern University in Ft. Lauderdale, Florida. He also has a M.S. Degree in Clinical Psychology from Nova University, a M.A. Degree in General-Experimental Psychology from Florida Atlantic University in Boca Raton, Florida and a B.A. Degree in Political Science from the University of South Carolina in Columbia, South Carolina.

Dr. Epstein has studied Happiness Research and Positive Psychology for the last 12 years and has written this book to help people become happier in their daily lives.

2Steps2Happiness:
It's Closer Than You Think

Dr. Adam M. Epstein

Published by Dr. Adam M. Epstein

This book is dedicated to my Parents for their years of support and encouragement.

Contents

Introduction: How to use this book

This book can be used in several different ways:

- Start at the beginning and read all the way through to the end.

- Go directly to a Section Heading of interest to you (e.g., Factors That Influence Your Level of Happiness, Social Interaction).

- Go directly to a Chapter which is of interest to you.

- Take the Epstein Happiness Inventory to assess your current status and what changes need to be made.

Regardless of how you approach this book, I suggest that you read **Section A: Factors That Influence Your Level of Happiness**. This section will explain the overall premise of 2Steps2Happiness.

Disclaimer

2Steps2Happiness is not intended as a substitute for psychotherapy. Any suggestions made by Dr. Epstein are not intended as a substitute for medical advice from a physician or psychotherapy from a mental health professional. Any individual who is experiencing severe emotional problems (i.e., suicidal thoughts, severe depression, hopelessness, hallucinations, delusions, etc.) is encouraged to seek immediate treatment from a qualified mental health practitioner and/or Call 911 or your local Crisis Line. The information provided is intended for educational purposes only, and is the opinion of the author.

Preface

Happiness in 2 steps? That sounds too good to be true. Surely, it must be more complicated than that. Well, I have spent over a decade pouring over Happiness Research Studies and have distilled it down to 2 steps.

The two steps are:

- Getting your needs met in a positive way and

- Dealing with life stressors in a positive way.

That's it!

Of course, these two steps beg several important questions:

- What is Happiness anyway?

- What human needs should I try to fulfill?

- What life stressors do humans often experience?

- What are the positive and negative ways that I'm trying to get my needs met and stressors dealt with?

The purpose of this book is to increase your level of happiness by helping you <u>avoid negative ways</u> (to get your needs met and deal with stressors) and instead <u>utilize positive ways</u> (to get your needs met and deal with stressors).

At this point, you may ask, **"Well, how is this book different than all the other books on Happiness out there?"**

Answers:

- **Practicality** - 2Steps2Happiness is nothing if not practical; concrete, doable suggestions are made throughout the book. Some other books tend to get bogged down in theory with limited applicability to people's real lives.

- **To the point** - Many non-fiction books, not just self-help books, tend to make their suppositions in page after page of elaboration and repetition. So many times, The basic point the author is making could be stated in one paragraph rather than 10 pages. That is what I have tried to do in this book - make points clearly and succinctly.

- **Comprehensive** - I have tried to cover all aspects of Happiness

Enhancement in this book; from human needs and stressors to emotions and physical sensations. I also incorporated cognitive, behavioral, and insight-oriented approaches to Happiness Enhancement.

- **Reality Based** - This book offers suggestions that psychologists have used for many years to help people become happier. These suggestions are derived from hundreds of clinical studies conducted over many years; they are based upon real-world applications, not made up in the head of one author.

You may also wonder, **"How can this book help me to be happier?"**

- It will dispel many of the myths of what makes people happy.

- It will help you assess your current ways of coping (both positive and negative).

- It offers numerous suggestions that you can tailor specifically to yourself (i.e., not one size fits all).

- It helps you to configure your own action plan for happiness enhancement.

- It's possible that you can learn more therapeutic techniques from this book than spending months or years in therapy.

- Bibliotherapy, which is the use of written materials to induce positive changes, has proven positive benefits as shown by many research studies. 2Steps2Happiness would certainly qualify as a great Bibliotherapy resource for you.

- 2Steps2Happiness is a versatile book that can be used in a variety of ways: For those of you interested in the whys (why do I act as I do), self-test inventories and insight-oriented chapters are available. Others may just be interested in finding solutions to current difficulties, and going directly to pertinent information. This book will be something you can read from beginning to end or as a reference book to be used as needed.

- A new expanded and updated chapter on Weight Loss/Management has been included in 2Steps2Happiness to address the overweight and obesity problems facing individuals worldwide.

Why I wrote this book

2Steps2Happiness teaches people to be happier in their daily lives. It is <u>not</u> psychotherapy, and does <u>not</u> utilize the medical model of diagnosis, illness, or medication. Instead, it focuses on teaching you to get your human needs met and to deal with life stressors in a positive, effective way. 2Steps2Happiness was created to address some of the deficiencies of today's mental health system. Let us look at some of the <u>facts</u> about Mental Health:

- A substantial majority of adults who experience emotional problems do not receive treatment. (See Chapter 6 of the Surgeon General's Report on Mental Health from 1999).

- Worry about costs was listed as the highest reason for not receiving treatment (Chapter 6 of the Surgeon General's Report on Mental Health from 1999).

- Stigma of receiving Mental Health Services still exists.

- HMO's focus on providing the least amount of Psychotherapy treatment and promoting less expensive drug treatment when possible (to improve their financial bottom line).

- The rate of depression, obesity, and financial debt has increased over the last 20 years.

- The medicalization of psychology (diagnosis, testing, symptoms, drugs) prevails.

- Over the past decade, Mental Health Professionals spend more time filling out paperwork and struggling with insurance companies and less time helping their clients.

The Bottom Line: There are a lot of people in this world who are unhappy and who receive no help from mental health providers to increase their level of happiness.

The Solution: I believe that something should be done to remedy this situation: Over the past century research has accumulated on why people experience emotional distress as well as what makes people happy. Most Americans have very little familiarity with this information. I believe that this information should be disseminated in an easy-to-understand, entertaining, and affordable fashion. In effect, the public should be taught about ways to be happier. Moreover, the focus of psychology should shift from a negative (i.e., illness, pathology, and disorder) to a positive one (learning skills, changing priorities, getting needs met, etc.). Ideally, the transition should be:

- From a **Negative** focus to a **Positive** focus
- From a focus on **Illness** to one of **Education**
- From **Stigma and Avoidance** to **A Quest for Knowledge**
- From using the term **Patient** to **Student**

I believe this approach should appeal to many individuals who would never go to a therapist. In fact, there has already been a shift towards the positive with the rise of the "Positive Psychology Movement" as well as an increase in "Personal and Executive Coaching ."

Of course, this does not mean all people should stop their psychotropic medications and/or quit seeing their therapist. Both of these services can be valuable in certain situations. 2Steps2Happiness is an attempt to help all those underserved people who could use some help but would never otherwise seek it. 2Steps2Happiness can also be a helpful adjunct to those people already receiving traditional mental health services.

Mission Statement

The mission of 2Steps2Happiness is to educate the public about ways to make their lives happier.

Who can Benefit from 2Steps2Happiness?

- People who are unhappy with the way they look or feel
- People who are stressed out, or unhappy with their relationships
- People who feel dissatisfied, anxious, sad, bored, lonely, or empty inside
- Anyone who wants to be Happier!

Benefits of Implementing 2Steps2Happiness:

- Improve your mood
- Age More Slowly
- Manage Your Money Better
- Sleep Better
- Enjoy Your Job
- Lose Weight
- Improve Your Health
- Improve Your Relationships

Just Some of What You Will Learn:

- To deal better with life stressors
- What research has shown about who is happy
- If money can buy happiness
- What brings meaning to your life
- What human needs should be fulfilled
- How your relationships with other people affect your happiness
- To design your own individualized "Action Plan" to guide your way to a happier life

"Happiness depends upon ourselves."
Aristotle

Chapter # 1: Common Myths of What Makes People Happy

Myth # 1: ***Young people are happier than older people.***
Reality: Actually some studies show that older people may be a little happier than their younger counterparts. (See the November, 1998 issue of the *Journal of Personality and Social Psychology* (Vol. 75, No. 5, p. 1333-1349).
Suggestion: If you are young, follow some of the suggestions given below. If you are older, you probably have learned to some extent how to regulate your emotions through experience.

Myth #2: ***Rich people are happier than non rich people.***
Reality: Surveys of life satisfaction conducted with rich, middle-class, and poor people found that rich people are not significantly happier than middle-class people. The rich do tend to be happier than poor people because poor people lack some of the basics.
Suggestion: Don't waste your life trying to be rich. Achieving middle-class status is sufficient; Making a lot of money will not necessarily make you any happier. Instead, spend more time nourishing your personal relationships.

Myth #3: ***Very intelligent people are happier than people who have average intelligence.***
Reality: Highly intelligent people appear to be no happier than people of average intelligence.
Suggestion: Don't worry if you're not Einstein.

Myth #4: ***Beautiful people are happier than average looking people.***
Reality: People who are very good-looking are no happier than average looking people.
Suggestion: Save your money on the plastic surgery.

Myth#5: ***People are happier if they can go from one exciting experience to another.***
Reality: Happy people are able to appreciate life's little pleasures (sunrise, clouds, birds, children, etc.)
Suggestion: You don't have to emulate James Bond to be happy.

Myth #6: ***Those lottery winners who don't have to work and can sit around eating snacks and watching T.V. have it made.***
Reality: Happy people engage in challenging activities, but they get enough rest (and sleep) as well. Either extreme (being over challenged or under challenged) will produce stress. In between these two states is an

ideal place where we feel challenged, but not overmatched.
Suggestion: Engage in meaningful activities and hobbies you enjoy.

Myth #7: Getting away from it all and meditating on a mountain top somewhere would be great.

Reality: That isolation may be fine for a few days or even weeks, but those people who report the greatest levels of happiness tend to be more social and enjoy good interpersonal relationships with other people (friends, family, lovers, etc.).

Suggestion: While it's true that people vary in how much social stimulation they need, socializing with others tends to provide most people with the best experiences of their lives and can help as a buffer against stress.

Myth #8: Happy people have rose-colored glasses on and don't see life as it really is.

Reality: There is a happy medium between optimism and realism.

Suggestion: Try to have a positive outlook, and have realistic expectations as well (Not always easy to do).

Myth #9: Happiness is 100% learned behavior.

Reality: Research indicates that happiness is about 50% genetic (nature) and 50% from our experiences (nurture).

Suggestion: Make the best of the 50% you can control.

Section A: Factors That Influence Your Level of Happiness

"People are about as happy as they make up their minds to be."

Abraham Lincoln

Chapter # 2: The Happiness Balloon

Think of your happiness level as a balloon. The happier you are the higher the balloon rises. The less happy you are, the lower the balloon sinks.

Balloon Altitude = Level of Happiness

Your happiness is composed of emotions and physical sensations.

Happiness = Emotions and Physical Sensations

Several factors affect the altitude of your happiness balloon. Think of stressors as sandbags. The more sandbags piled on your balloon, the lower your balloon sinks.

Sandbags = Stressors

Also, if you don't get your needs met, your balloon will sink. Fulfilling your needs is the same as properly inflating your balloon with Helium.

Helium (more raises balloon, less lowers balloon) = Getting Needs met in a positive way increases amount of Helium

Using positive coping styles will help raise your balloon by throwing off sand bags and helping you meet your needs.

Positive Coping Styles = dispose of sandbags and increase amount of Helium

Negative Coping Styles are like hypodermic needles. Injecting your balloon will temporarily raise your level, but when you pull the needle out, a hole will be left, and in the long run you will sink due to "slow leaks."

Negative Coping Styles = Hypodermic needles gives temporary lift, but long-term drop

Definition of Factors

Need Fulfillment - Like all biological organisms, Human Beings have basic needs which must be fulfilled in order to survive. Examples of the most basic needs would be air or water. Beyond these physiological needs are "higher order" or more abstract needs which also need to be fulfilled. (Examples include social needs, existential (meaning of life) needs, relaxation needs, identity needs, etc.) See Chapter # 3 for A Detailed Explanation of Basic Human Needs.

Life Stressors - Stressors are those events, situations, or relationships which most people perceive as difficult or unpleasant. (Examples include relationship difficulties, financial problems, unemployment, retirement, illness, etc.) See Chapter # 4 for A List of Life Stressors.

Negative Coping Styles - Ways of behaving or thinking which are emotionally, physically, financially, or socially harmful to an individual or his/her associates. (Examples include alcohol abuse, drug abuse, overeating, compulsive gambling, compulsive working, etc.) See Chapter # 5 for A List of Negative Coping Styles.

Positive Coping Styles - Ways of behaving or thinking which are emotionally, physically, financially, or socially helpful to an individual by helping him/her cope with stress and fulfill his/her needs. See Appendix # 2 for a list of Positive Coping Styles.

Emotions - A state of consciousness relating to the arousal of feelings. Emotions can be positive, negative, or neutral. (Examples include boredom, anger, sadness, joy, etc.) See Chapter # 6 for A List of Human Emotions and Reasons we have Emotions.

Physical Sensations - Bodily experiences perceived by an individual. These sensations can be positive, negative, or neutral. (Examples include back pain, headaches, dizziness, fatigue, etc.) See Chapter # 7 for A List of Negative Physical Sensations.

Interaction of Factors

When **Human Needs** go unfulfilled, **Negative Emotions** and/or **Negative Physical Sensations** may occur

> (For example, if the **Human Need**, Sleep goes unfulfilled, the **Negative Physical Sensation**, Fatigue will occur).

Individuals may use **Negative Coping Styles** to try and fulfill **Human Needs** which can lead to **Stressors**.

> (For example, a person may use the **Negative Coping Style**, compulsive gambling to fulfill his **Human Need**, for Stimulation. This coping style may cause the **Stressor**, Financial Problems).

Life Stressors are an inevitable part of life. Compounded **Stressors** (i.e., experiencing several **Stressors** at the same time) usually are more difficult to cope with than individual ones.

> (For example, personal illness, marital problems, and financial

difficulties all occurring at the same time).

Experiencing **Life Stressors** may cause **Negative Emotions** and/or **Negative Physical Sensations**

(For example, the **Life Stressor**, <u>personal illness</u> may promote the **Negative Emotion**, <u>sadness</u>).

People use both **Negative** and **Positive Coping Styles** to deal with **Stressors**.

(For example, a person could use the **Negative Coping Style**, <u>physical aggression</u>, or the **Positive Coping Style**, <u>communication skills</u>, to deal with the **Stressor**, relationship problems).

Using **Negative Coping Styles** may temporarily relieve **Stressors** in the short-term, but may be harmful in the long-term.

(For example, a person may use the **Negative Coping Style**, <u>alcohol abuse</u>, to relieve the **Stressor**, <u>death of a friend</u>, but the temporary pain relief could lead to addiction, health or relationship problems).

GOAL: Using **Positive Coping Styles** instead of **Negative Coping Styles** to **Fulfill Your Needs** and cope with **Life Stressors** should lead to **Positive Emotions** and **Positive Sensations (i.e., an elevated Happiness Balloon).**

At this point you may ask, "Now that I understand what the factors are, and how they interact, how do I use this information to increase my level of Happiness?"

Take the Epstein Happiness Inventory on Page 27 to assess:

- What Negative Emotions you are experiencing
- What Negative Physical Sensations you are experiencing
- What Stressors you are experiencing
- What Negative Coping Styles you are using
- Which Human Needs are going unfulfilled

After taking the Epstein Happiness Inventory, you will have a better idea of your status and can make appropriate changes in your life. Periodically, you can re-take the Epstein Happiness Inventory to illustrate how learning new Positive Coping Styles has *decreased* negative emotions, negative physical sensations, and negative coping styles.

Keep the following in mind when implementing New Coping Styles:

- Perseverance pays off. Keep trying to use positive coping styles. Change may be slow and there will probably be setbacks, but perseverance usually pays off and you will eventually achieve your happiness goals.

- Try different positive coping styles, and see what works best for you.

- Weigh the pros and cons of your choices to get a better idea of potential benefits and/or consequences of your next step. (Hint: Write them out on two columns on a piece of paper.)

- Your basic personality (temperament) will probably not change radically over your lifetime. Personality is formed by your genetic make-up and early experiences. This does not mean that you cannot change, but realistically, you will probably be able to change only within certain limitations. However, people do tend to "mellow" with age; meaning that they are able to regulate their emotions better as they get older.

- The only person you can change is yourself. Don't waist your time trying to change others. You can only change your own thoughts and behaviors; not others.

- Knowing the reasons why you act the way you do (i.e., psychological insight) <u>May</u> or <u>May Not</u> help you change your behaviors/thinking currently.

- There are times when you must extract yourself from your environment (e.g., ending a relationship, etc.) to reduce stress levels.

- Repetition is a great way to learn something new and remember it.

- Try to change the things you can (within your power) and accept those things you cannot or will not change.

- Things in life eventually change whether you want them to change or not.

- You are probably using many Positive Coping Styles already. See Appendix # 2 for a list of the Positive Coping Styles you are using currently. Give yourself credit for using these styles.

Chapter # 3 : A Detailed Explanation of Basic Human Needs

<u>Physiological needs</u> - These are the most basic needs of human beings and many other animals as well. Fulfillment of these needs is necessary for life itself. When these needs are not regularly fulfilled, it is difficult to think of higher order needs (e.g., Existential issues).

- Air (breathing)
- Water
- Food
- Shelter, safety & security
- Urination and defecation
- Sleep

- **Absence of pain** - Both physical and emotional pain are warning signs that something is wrong. Pain can be a great motivator and forces people to take action even when they don't want to. People will go to great lengths to avoid pain. Pain avoidance runs the gamut from taking aspirin to suicide as a way to stop pain.

- **Sex** - Sex is a very primitive urge which motivates us to procreate. This strong desire can often supersede rational thought. Some evolutionary psychologists (and psychoanalysts as well) believe that many human behaviors are overtly or covertly influenced by the sex drive. This viewpoint may have some merit, as the very survival and continuation of our species depends upon sexual reproduction. Those behaviors which promote reproduction, child birth, and cultivation of the child until he/she can reproduce, are passed along to the next generation (and their genes as well). Conversely, if a person exhibits behaviors which inhibit reproduction, those genes will not be passed down to the next generation.

<u>Social needs</u>

- **To have at least one consistent relationship where there is sharing, caring, empathy, concern, self-disclosure, and give-and-take** - This is probably one of the most important needs of all. It is vital in childhood through old age. A child's current and future mental health depends a lot on having such a relationship. Having this relationship helps us cope with life stressors and can contribute to our happiness. Such a relationship can be with a parent, relative, friend, or romantic partner.

- **To communicate/socialize with others** - Human beings are truly social creatures. Unlike some other solitary animals like tigers, we need contact with others to survive. We feel compelled to share our thoughts and feelings both verbally and non-verbally with others. Most of our best experiences are usually those shared with others. The opposite of socializing is being alone. That's why solitary confinement is considered one of the worst punishments society can dole out.

- **To nurture and care for others (e.g., children, spouses, siblings)** - Most parents instinctively nurture their children. Such nurturance or caring can extend as well to other family members, friends, and sometimes even to strangers. Just think of the shock people experience when they hear of rare occurrences when parents abandon or neglect their children. It seems unnatural.

- **To be listened to and understood** - When people talk, they want to be truly heard and understood. If you doubt this, just think of the times you have spoken, and someone has talked right over you, or their response has nothing to do with what you just said; or the times people have listened but don't understand what you are talking about. These are frustrating situations. Conversely, think of the people you have spoken to that are good listeners and can understand exactly what you are saying. Talking to such a person can be very gratifying. When people communicate, they want to know that what they are saying is being received and understood.

- **To know what others (e.g., friends, celebrities, etc.) are up to** - People are inherently "yentas" or busybodies. They love to know what others are up to. Evidence of this is all around us. When there is a traffic accident, the "rubberneckers" want to see what's happening. At every office or organization, people constantly talk about each other (gossip). This phenomenon extends to the mass media as well (i.e., the appeal of soap operas and tabloid newspapers).

- **To be attractive to the opposite sex (or in some cases, same sex)** - Both men and women primp and prepare to be appealing. Whether it's clothing, sports cars, jewelry, make-up, dieting, or bodybuilding, all these behaviors try to enhance our appearance for someone else.

Balancing Act - Achieving a balance in life is not easy. It is necessary, though, to promote our happiness and the happiness of others.

- **People need to alternate between relaxation and stimulation** - People tend to get bored or stressed out when they experience the same level of stimulation consistently for any length of time. When you are bombarded by stimulating events, sounds, or sights for a while, you will crave some relaxation. Conversely, if you are in a relaxing, invariable, environment for a while, you will crave some stimulation. This is also why people like vacations; to break up the monotony. Novel environments can be stimulating. People utilize many things to change their level of stimulation (drugs, music, movies, etc.) as a way to be relaxed or aroused.

- **People like to be led (e.g., by political leaders), and to be free (liberty to do what we want)** - Most human societies establish hierarchies where one or a few humans are in charge, with others in subordinate positions. Hierarchies tend to reduce conflicts. Most humans like having a "strong" leader who gives them direction, leadership, and stability. But, people also like "doing their own thing" too. They like the freedom to do what they want to do, when they want to do it. There is a constant struggle between these two forces and either extreme causes problems (i.e., dictatorships or anarchy). The same struggle occurs on an individual level. As a child grows up he requires structure, direction, and supervision. As he grows older he craves more freedom to do what he wants. In adult relationships, people like an effective leader at work, but don't want to be over controlled. In some religions, people struggle between the dictates of their "leader" and their own desires.

- **To be accepted by the "crowd," and to be individuals** - People also struggle between being accepted by others and being unique individuals. The desired acceptance of others drives many people's behaviors. They want positive regard from their parents, teachers, and friends. They will alter their behaviors to "fit in" with their peers. Rejection by others (i.e., ostracism) is very disturbing to most people. Conversely, people want their own identities. They want to be unique and have their own thoughts, beliefs, and feelings. They take pride in being different or "better" than the masses. Of course, people usually express their uniqueness within some parameters. If they act too differently, they may be ostracized.

- **To work for our own self-interest, and to cooperate with others** - Humans constantly struggle with meeting their own needs versus helping others. Of course, either extreme is problematic. Being "selfish" is looked down upon by most people; Just doing things for others while not taking care of your own needs is counterproductive as well. Since most people live with others around, they must learn to cooperate, compromise, negotiate, and give to others. It is essential to the survival of our species. In many cases we enjoy helping others (i.e., nurturing children, helping friends, etc.). Keeping a balance between doing for ourselves and doing for others can be difficult, but it is necessary.

<u>Existential Issues</u> - These are issues that deal with meaning and death.

- **To explore and make sense of our world** - Human beings both as individuals and groups attempt to explore and make sense of the world. The human infant is constantly trying to do this. On a much larger scale, the dawn of Homo Sapiens emerging from Africa and spreading throughout the world was driven by this need. Scientific inquiry and exploration of the earth and cosmos is also driven by this need. Humans crave explanations for how and why things work, and what is beyond the next horizon.

- **To have identity (Who am I?)** - People struggle to know who they really are. They attempt to acquire their own beliefs and values, not necessarily those of their family, friends, culture, etc. People define their identity by talking with other non-judgmental people, trying new activities, reading, etc. Identity can also be defined by one's *role* (mother, father, husband, wife, brother, sister, son, daughter), *religion* (Christian, Jew, etc.) *nationality* (American, Mexican, etc.) *heritage* (Irish, Italian, etc.) *job* (plumber, housewife, engineer, etc.), and *family background* (e.g., I'm a 4th generation McCoy originally from Ireland, etc.). Traditions and rituals also give people identity. People use all of these criteria to define who they are.

- **To be creative (both a creator & consumer of other's creations)** - For at least 30,000 years, humans have been creating works of art and appreciating other people's creativity. Creativity can be art, architecture, music, photography, writing, poetry, stories, etc. If you don't enjoy creating, then you probably are a consumer of other people's works. Watching movies, TV, reading books, going to an art museum, are all examples of "art" appreciation. Creativity is not confined to classical arts. It can also be coming up with innovative ideas, gardening, or any hobby that utilizes your imagination at work or home.

- **To avoid death** - Everyone knows that one day they will die. Such knowledge is anxiety provoking to say the least. People deal with this knowledge differently. Most people live in denial about it, especially when they are young. Survival is a very strong instinct. That is why suicidal behavior is considered by many to be "crazy." Some people feel that when they die, they will go to an afterlife. Such beliefs alleviate some of their death anxiety.

<u>Miscellaneous</u>

- **To have control of ourselves and our environment** - This is a very important human need. People like stability. We like to believe that our actions will lead to predictable results, (i.e., that we control our destinies). The unknown and unpredictable are very scary and anxiety provoking. Unexpected and uncontrollable events like earthquakes, lightning, and tornadoes scare us as they did early man. Research indicates that "healthy" people actually overestimate how much control they have over their lives. Just think of all the major events that people have no control over (Their genetic makeup, who raises them as children, whether they are born in a wealthy or poor country, diseases, accidents, etc.). Of course, this does not mean that we have no control over our lives. There are many steps we can take to give our lives predictability. People who feel like they have no control over their destinies usually feel either depressed or anxious or both. It seems that the perception of control may be more important than actual control. Religion helps some people feel that either they (through prayer) or god (through divine intervention) has control over their destiny. In either case, there is a belief that if one does and/or believes certain tenets, a predictable result will follow. Such beliefs reduce anxiety for some people. Moreover, people like someone who will <u>always</u> be there for them, accepting of them, and interested in them.

- **To possess territory** - Men, like other animals, are territorial beings. We have killed and are killing millions of people over land rights. Wars to acquire land have been around since the dawn of man. In general, people are very possessive over their property and possessions.

<u>Vicarious Need Fulfillment</u>

- As you can see from the above materials, people have many needs to be fulfilled. Sometimes, for a variety of reasons, people may not be able to (or want to) meet these needs directly. In those cases, people will meet these needs vicariously. For example, the need, "To nurture and care for others" usually concerns nurturing other people. As many people know, **pets** (See Chapter # 35) can be an excellent substitute for people. Sometimes people use television, movies, or books as a substitute for social interaction. This vicarious "social interaction" can be somewhat helpful, but is still not as good as the "real thing."

"Even a happy life cannot be without a measure of darkness, and the word happy would lose its meaning if it were not balanced by sadness."

Carl Jung

Chapter # 4 : Life Stressors

Indecision - Not being able to make up your mind about something or issues that remained unresolved for a long time (i.e., limbo).

Interpersonal Conflicts - Such conflicts can be in the form of:

- Negative communication (criticism from others)
- Distorted communication (having unrealistic expectations of others)
- Non-communication (withdrawal from others)

Types of interpersonal conflict include the following:

- Conjugal (marital or nonmarital) - discord, separation, divorce, unfaithfulness
- Relatives - parent-child, siblings, other relatives
- Problems with friends, neighbors, associates, boss, coworkers

Developmental - Life transitions or phases of the life cycle

Examples include:

- Entering school
- Puberty
- Graduation
- Transition from adolescent to adult
- Starting a new career
- Engagement
- Marriage
- Becoming a parent
- Children leaving home
- Menopause
- Retirement
- Age-related cognitive decline

Illness

- Being the caretaker of a physically or mentally incapacitated person
- Personal or familial illness (acute or chronic), injury, accident, surgery, abortion.

Occupational - which includes either Work, School, or Homemaking

- Being fired or laid off from work
- Chronic Unemployment
- Academic Problems (failing grades, underachievement)

- Job dissatisfaction
- Uncertainty about career choices

Living Circumstances

- Changes in residence, or threats to your personal safety

Financial difficulties

- Inadequate finances (i.e., not enough money to pay the bills)
- Change in financial status (i.e., moving from rich to poor, poor to rich, etc.)

Legal - arrest, imprisonment, lawsuit, trial, court appearance

Abuse - Recipient of verbal, physical, or sexual abuse

Acculturation Problem - Problem involving adjustment to a different culture following migration.

Identity Problem - uncertainty about identity such as long-term goals, career choice, sexual orientation and behavior, or moral values.

Death of a spouse, close family member or friend.

Other - Natural or manmade disaster, persecution, unwanted pregnancy, rape.

Chapter # 5: Negative Coping Styles

Negative coping styles can vary in the degree and frequency that they are used. Using them chronically can lead to harmful consequences.

For example, avoiding others periodically can be a way to relax. Withdrawing from others chronically can be problematic.

Sometimes, these coping styles are used as a source of **stimulation** (See Chapter #43) or **relaxation** (See Chapter # 38).

Below are a list of Coping Styles that people use to stimulate/relax themselves, deal with stressors, or help them fulfill needs. Remember these styles can be *problematic* if they interfere with your social, emotional, financial, occupational, physical, or academic functioning.

Potentially Problematic Behaviors:

- Alcohol Use
- Illicit Drugs
- Prescription Drugs
- Overeating
- Under eating
- Compulsive Cleaning/Organizing
- Compulsive Ritualistic Behaviors
- Compulsive Sex
- Sleeping Too Much
- Compulsive Gambling
- Compulsive Shopping/Spending
- Working too much
- Compulsive Exercising
- Vomiting (self-induced)
- Purposely cutting yourself with a sharp object to "feel" something or **distract** (See Chapter # 44) yourself
- Acting impulsively too often
- Excessive Procrastination
- Suicidal gestures
- Experiencing a lot of pain for which the doctors cannot find a cause
- Feeling emotionally "numb" (dissociation)
- Difficulty showing and/or feeling emotion
- Difficulty trying new things
- Being overly Perfectionistic
- Frequent Temper Tantrums

Problematic Interpersonal Behaviors:

- Being overly critical of others
- Saying YES to others when you should say NO
- Avoiding others too much
- Being overly verbally aggressive with others
- Being overly physically aggressive with others
- Being too "clingy" with others
- Blaming others for your own mistakes
- Deliberately annoying others
- Staying in an abusive relationship
- Repeatedly lying to others
- Dropping all your friends when you get a romantic partner
- Not being a good listener
- Not having good manners
- Not initiating conversations when you should
- Bragging
- Being overly sexually flirtatious
- Being overly protective of others

Chapter # 6: Human Emotions and Reasons We Have Them

Why do we have emotions (feelings)?

Ultimately, all emotional states are physiological in nature. Thoughts and feelings are neural activity of the brain. Evolution may have designed them as a way of motivating humans to do the things they need to do to reproduce and survive. Facial expression of emotions can also be a method of communication to others. Emotions can emerge as a reaction to outside forces (i.e., your environment) or inner forces (hunger, hormones, etc.).

What are some typical emotions?

Affectionate	Aggressive	Agonized	Angry	Annoyed
Anxious	Apathetic	Apologetic	Arrogant	Bashful
Betrayed	Blissful	Blue	Bored	Burdened
Cautious	Charmed	Cheated	Cheerful	Concentrating
Condemned	Confident	Conflicted	Confused	Contented
Crushed	Curious	Defeated	Depressed	Despairing
Determined	Disappointed	Disapproving	Disbelieving	Discouraged
Disgusted	Dissatisfied	Distractible	Distraught	Disturbed
Dominated	Eager	Ecstatic	Empathetic	Empty
Energetic	Enraged	Enthusiastic	Envious	Exasperated
Excited	Exhausted	Exploitive	Evil	Failure
Fearful	Foolish	Flustered	Forgetful	Frantic
Frightened	Frustrated	Grief-stricken	Guilty	Happy
Helpful	Helpless	High	Hopeful	Hopeless
Horrible	Hurt	Hypervigilant	Hysterical	Idiotic
Ignored	Imposed upon	Impulsive	Indifferent	Indecisive
Infuriated	Innocent	Interested	Intimidated	Irritable
Isolated	Jealous	Jumpy	Kind	Lazy
Left-Out	Lonely	Loving	Lovestruck	Manic
Meditative	Melancholy	Mischievous	Miserable	Mood Swings
Negative	Nervous	Obstinate	Okay	Optimistic
Outraged	Pained	Panicky	Paranoid	Peaceful
Perfectionistic	Perplexed	Persecuted	Pressured	Prudish
Punished	Put-Upon	Puzzled	Rageful	Regretful
Rejected	Relaxed	Relieved	Restless	Sad

Satisfied	Scared	Sheepish	Shocked	Sleepy
Smug	Spiteful	Stunned	Stupid	Surly
Surprised	Sympathetic	Tense	Terrible	Terrified
Thwarted	Tired	Trapped	Troubled	Ugly
Unhappy	Uninterested	Unmotivated	Vulnerable	Wonderful
Weepy	Worried	Worthless		

How do people express emotions?

- Verbally - This is the basis for most psychotherapy; Talking about feelings and problems. By talking to an empathetic, non-judgmental person, we vent our feelings or "get it off our chest". This also gives us the opportunity to sort out issues in our minds.

- Using the written word - Writing down our thoughts and feelings is a form of expression. Sometimes it is easier to clarify issues when we see them in black and white on paper. Writing down the pros and cons of a decision or keeping a "feelings journal" are common forms of written expression.

- Artistic expression (poetry, painting, sculpture, music) - Expressing oneself artistically can serve the same function as talking or writing.

- Movement of the body - Such expression can take the form of Dance, Yoga (as a method of relaxation) or exercise (as a way to reduce stress and/or gain competence in a skill (e.g., martial arts, tennis, etc.).

Bottling up feelings.

In general, it is not beneficial to bottle up your feelings. If things are bothering you, it helps to talk about these feelings with someone you trust. If you don't, it can harm you both physically and/or psychologically. It is beneficial to recognize and identify feelings as they occur. When you can do this, you can then attempt to change them, if you choose. Knowing how *you really feel*, not how others want or think you should feel, is of the utmost importance. Sometimes parents discourage their children from expressing their true feelings or, in some cases, expressing any feelings. When these children grow up, they may:

- Not know how they really feel

- Be "cut off" or dissociated from their feelings

- Be afraid if they do experience strong feelings, that they will become overwhelmed and won't be able to stop these emotions

- Develop a "coat of armor," which insulates them and does not allow them to experience strong feelings.

Who is the best person to express your feelings to?

Someone who is a good listener, empathetic, and non-judgmental. It is in this environment that people can experience, sort out, and express their true feelings.

How do we change our feelings /mood?

Basically, we can change our mood by:

- Expressing our thoughts and feelings (See above).
- Changing our behaviors.
- Changing our thinking.
- Changing our environment.
- Learning new skills.

Put on a happy face.

Some research studies indicate that pretending to be happy (i.e., moving the muscles of your face into a smile) may actually activate and promote positive feelings. In effect, it is the reverse of the process we usually experience where we feel good, and subsequently smile. The premise is that moving those facial muscles will bring on the feelings usually associated with them. (See Laird, James, (1974). Expressive face changes emotions. Journal of Personality and Social Psychology, 29, 475-486).

Mood swings or alternating feelings.

For most people, both good and bad moods rarely last for long. Moods change with positive and negative events that occur around us; Neutral or contented mood usually returns with time. In general, the worst emotional consequences of bad, or even horrible events are usually temporary. Recuperation or rebound will usually occur over time. In fact, horrible events may even cause one to change their priorities and/or values, and appreciate life more. Even very positive events have only a temporary impact on mood; The "high" will fade.

Most people experience similar feelings, thoughts, and behaviors throughout their lifetime (love, jealousy, caring, etc.). People vary in how often they experience certain feelings, the intensity of such feelings, and how much their mood fluctuates. Some people experience extremes of mood (i.e., mood swings) or negative mood for long periods of time. The reasons why some individuals experience mood swings probably derives from biological and environmental causes.

What to do when feeling overwhelmed by continuous, unwanted, intense emotions.

** You may want to consult a mental health professional, but the following may be helpful **

- **Name or label the emotion**. This may not be as easy as you think. Sometimes people feel general emotional turmoil, but don't know exactly what the precise feeling is that they are experiencing. Being able to label the emotion can help reduce the turmoil surrounding it. (See the first part of this Chapter for a list of emotions).

- Note if there are any **physical sensations** (See Chapter # 7) associated with the feelings.

- After understanding the precise feelings you are experiencing (and any physical sensations that accompany these feelings), the next step is to accept these feelings as legitimate (after all, they are *your feelings* whether they are "logical" or not). Try not to get caught up in whether most people feel this way in this situation, or that you are "wrong" to feel the way you do. Such self-condemnation only makes you feel worse. Just because you feel a certain way doesn't mean you have to act on it.

- Try to identify what may have triggered this feeling. Is there a certain situation, event, person, or place that elicits this feeling? Is there an internal state (e.g., hunger, tiredness, menstruation, etc.) that triggers such feelings?

- What were your thoughts or **expectations** (See Chapter # 27) surrounding the situation/trigger. For example, if you expect all automobile drivers to behave courteously on the road, you will certainly get angry when they don't. If you don't expect this, then you may not react as strongly. In other words, the expectations you have affect how you respond to a situation.

- Think about how you usually respond to the trigger or feelings elicited from the trigger. How do you act? What do you say? How would you prefer to respond in that situation?

- Acknowledge that this is only a feeling, and although it's distressful, it can't hurt you or cause any lasting danger. At times, you may want to gradually become **detached** from (See Chapter # 44) your feelings and thoughts to feel safer if you are overwhelmed.

- Identify other ways to deal with such feelings. (See Appendix # 2: Positive Coping Styles).

"Three grand essentials to happiness in this life are something to do, something to love, and something to hope for."

Joseph Addison

Chapter # 7: Negative Physical Sensations

People experience negative physical sensations for a variety of reasons; illness, diet, lack of sleep, stress, anxiety, depression, etc. It is helpful to know the source of these sensations and to investigate whether unmet needs or stressors are contributing to these sensations. A first step is to rule out a physical cause to any negative sensations you are experiencing by paying a visit to your physician (See Chapter # 37). If no physical cause seems apparent, then taking the **Epstein Happiness Inventory** below may give you some insight into the derivation of your negative physical sensations. Below are a list of common negative physical sensations.

Abdominal pain	Agitation
Appetite reduction	Back pain
Bowel disturbance (diarrhea/constipation)	Breathing difficulty
Choking feeling	Burning or itching skin
Chest pains	Chills
Clenched teeth	Compulsive behaviors (pulling hair, biting fingernails)
Crying	Dizziness
Don't like being touched	Dry mouth
Excessive sweating (not due to heat)	Fainting spells
Fatigue	Fear of dying
Fear of losing control	Flushes (feeling hot)
Headaches	Hearing problems
High blood pressure	Incoordination
Lightheadedness	Muscle tension
Muscle tics	Muscles spasms
Numbness	Palpitations (heart pounding or fluttering)
Rapid heartbeat	Skin problems

Spaced out feeling (like things are unreal)	Tingling
Tremors (hand trembling)	Unsteady walking or balance
Visual disturbances	Vomiting

Epstein Happiness Inventory

The purpose of the following Inventory is to assess five factors that affect your level of happiness. These five factors are Negative Emotions, Negative Physical Sensations, Stressors, Negative Coping Styles, and Need Fulfillment. By completing this somewhat lengthy Happiness Inventory, you will establish: 1) What <u>Negative Emotions</u> you have experienced in recent times and how intense these feelings have been. Numerous descriptive words have been provided to help you define precisely how you feel. Sometimes, just defining how we feel can help us to feel better. 2) What <u>Negative Physical Sensations</u> you may have experienced recently which may be related to your emotional status. 3) What <u>Stressors</u> you have experienced. Sometimes, people don't realize how many stressors they have experienced without seeing a list and identifying them. 4) What <u>Negative Coping Styles</u> you may have used or currently use to deal with stressors or try to get your needs met. 5) What <u>Needs</u> are not being fulfilled. This will give you a better idea if you are fulfilling your human needs and whether you need to work on getting unmet needs fulfilled.

You may also consider taking this Inventory again in the future to assess areas of improvement and areas which still need to be addressed.

Factor 1: Negative Emotions - Below, in the left column, are a list of negative emotions. If you have <u>not</u> experienced this emotion in recent months, do <u>not</u> circle any number in the right column. If you <u>have</u> experienced this emotion in recent months, circle a number from 1-10. The higher the number, the more intense the emotion has been (Ex. 1-bothers me a little, 5-bothers me a moderate amount, 10-bothers me a great deal).

EMOTION	INTENSITY OF EMOTION
Aggressive	1 2 3 4 5 6 7 8 9 10
Agonized	1 2 3 4 5 6 7 8 9 10
Angry	1 2 3 4 5 6 7 8 9 10
Annoyed	1 2 3 4 5 6 7 8 9 10
Anxious	1 2 3 4 5 6 7 8 9 10
Apathetic	1 2 3 4 5 6 7 8 9 10
Arrogant	1 2 3 4 5 6 7 8 9 10
Betrayed	1 2 3 4 5 6 7 8 9 10
Blue	1 2 3 4 5 6 7 8 9 10

EMOTION	INTENSITY OF EMOTION
Bored	1 2 3 4 5 6 7 8 9 10
Burdened	1 2 3 4 5 6 7 8 9 10
Cautious	1 2 3 4 5 6 7 8 9 10
Cheated	1 2 3 4 5 6 7 8 9 10
Conflicted	1 2 3 4 5 6 7 8 9 10
Confused	1 2 3 4 5 6 7 8 9 10
Crushed	1 2 3 4 5 6 7 8 9 10
Defeated	1 2 3 4 5 6 7 8 9 10
Depressed	1 2 3 4 5 6 7 8 9 10
Despairing	1 2 3 4 5 6 7 8 9 10
Disappointed	1 2 3 4 5 6 7 8 9 10
Disbelieving	1 2 3 4 5 6 7 8 9 10
Discouraged	1 2 3 4 5 6 7 8 9 10
Disgusted	1 2 3 4 5 6 7 8 9 10
Dissatisfied	1 2 3 4 5 6 7 8 9 10
Distractible	1 2 3 4 5 6 7 8 9 10
Distraught	1 2 3 4 5 6 7 8 9 10
Disturbed	1 2 3 4 5 6 7 8 9 10
Dominated	1 2 3 4 5 6 7 8 9 10
Empty	1 2 3 4 5 6 7 8 9 10
Enraged	1 2 3 4 5 6 7 8 9 10
Envious	1 2 3 4 5 6 7 8 9 10
Exasperated	1 2 3 4 5 6 7 8 9 10
Exhausted	1 2 3 4 5 6 7 8 9 10
Exploitive	1 2 3 4 5 6 7 8 9 10
Evil	1 2 3 4 5 6 7 8 9 10

EMOTION	INTENSITY OF EMOTION
Failure	1 2 3 4 5 6 7 8 9 10
Fearful	1 2 3 4 5 6 7 8 9 10
Foolish	1 2 3 4 5 6 7 8 9 10
Flustered	1 2 3 4 5 6 7 8 9 10
Forgetful	1 2 3 4 5 6 7 8 9 10
Frantic	1 2 3 4 5 6 7 8 9 10
Frightened	1 2 3 4 5 6 7 8 9 10
Frustrated	1 2 3 4 5 6 7 8 9 10
Grief-stricken	1 2 3 4 5 6 7 8 9 10
Guilty	1 2 3 4 5 6 7 8 9 10
Helpless	1 2 3 4 5 6 7 8 9 10
Hopeless	1 2 3 4 5 6 7 8 9 10
Horrible	1 2 3 4 5 6 7 8 9 10
Hurt	1 2 3 4 5 6 7 8 9 10
Hypervigilant	1 2 3 4 5 6 7 8 9 10
Hysterical	1 2 3 4 5 6 7 8 9 10
Idiotic	1 2 3 4 5 6 7 8 9 10
Ignored	1 2 3 4 5 6 7 8 9 10
Imposed upon	1 2 3 4 5 6 7 8 9 10
Impulsive	1 2 3 4 5 6 7 8 9 10
Indifferent	1 2 3 4 5 6 7 8 9 10
Indecisive	1 2 3 4 5 6 7 8 9 10
Infuriated	1 2 3 4 5 6 7 8 9 10
Intimidated	1 2 3 4 5 6 7 8 9 10
Irritable	1 2 3 4 5 6 7 8 9 10
Isolated	1 2 3 4 5 6 7 8 9 10

EMOTION	INTENSITY OF EMOTION
Jealous	1 2 3 4 5 6 7 8 9 10
Jumpy	1 2 3 4 5 6 7 8 9 10
Lazy	1 2 3 4 5 6 7 8 9 10
Left Out	1 2 3 4 5 6 7 8 9 10
Lonely	1 2 3 4 5 6 7 8 9 10
Manic	1 2 3 4 5 6 7 8 9 10
Melancholy	1 2 3 4 5 6 7 8 9 10
Miserable	1 2 3 4 5 6 7 8 9 10
Mood Swings	1 2 3 4 5 6 7 8 9 10
Negative	1 2 3 4 5 6 7 8 9 10
Nervous	1 2 3 4 5 6 7 8 9 10
Obstinate	1 2 3 4 5 6 7 8 9 10
Outraged	1 2 3 4 5 6 7 8 9 10
Pained	1 2 3 4 5 6 7 8 9 10
Panicky	1 2 3 4 5 6 7 8 9 10
Paranoid	1 2 3 4 5 6 7 8 9 10
Perfectionistic	1 2 3 4 5 6 7 8 9 10
Perplexed	1 2 3 4 5 6 7 8 9 10
Persecuted	1 2 3 4 5 6 7 8 9 10
Pressured	1 2 3 4 5 6 7 8 9 10
Punished	1 2 3 4 5 6 7 8 9 10
Put Upon	1 2 3 4 5 6 7 8 9 10
Puzzled	1 2 3 4 5 6 7 8 9 10
Rageful	1 2 3 4 5 6 7 8 9 10
Regretful	1 2 3 4 5 6 7 8 9 10
Rejected	1 2 3 4 5 6 7 8 9 10

EMOTION	INTENSITY OF EMOTION
Restless	1 2 3 4 5 6 7 8 9 10
Sad	1 2 3 4 5 6 7 8 9 10
Scared	1 2 3 4 5 6 7 8 9 10
Shocked	1 2 3 4 5 6 7 8 9 10
Sleepy	1 2 3 4 5 6 7 8 9 10
Spiteful	1 2 3 4 5 6 7 8 9 10
Stunned	1 2 3 4 5 6 7 8 9 10
Stupid	1 2 3 4 5 6 7 8 9 10
Surly	1 2 3 4 5 6 7 8 9 10
Tense	1 2 3 4 5 6 7 8 9 10
Terrible	1 2 3 4 5 6 7 8 9 10
Terrified	1 2 3 4 5 6 7 8 9 10
Thwarted	1 2 3 4 5 6 7 8 9 10
Tired	1 2 3 4 5 6 7 8 9 10
Trapped	1 2 3 4 5 6 7 8 9 10
Troubled	1 2 3 4 5 6 7 8 9 10
Ugly	1 2 3 4 5 6 7 8 9 10
Unhappy	1 2 3 4 5 6 7 8 9 10
Uninterested	1 2 3 4 5 6 7 8 9 10
Unmotivated	1 2 3 4 5 6 7 8 9 10
Vulnerable	1 2 3 4 5 6 7 8 9 10
Weepy	1 2 3 4 5 6 7 8 9 10
Worried	1 2 3 4 5 6 7 8 9 10
Worthless	1 2 3 4 5 6 7 8 9 10

Factor 2: Negative Physical Sensations

Below, in the left column, are a list of negative physical sensations. If you have not experienced this sensation in recent months, do not circle any number in the right column. If you have experienced this sensation in recent months, circle a number from 1-10. The higher the number, the more intense the sensation has been (Ex. 1-bothers me a little, 5-bothers me a moderate amount, 10-bothers me a great deal).

PHYSICAL SENSATION	INTENSITY OF SENSATIONS
Abdominal Pain	1 2 3 4 5 6 7 8 9 10
Agitation	1 2 3 4 5 6 7 8 9 10
Appetite reduction	1 2 3 4 5 6 7 8 9 10
Back Pain	1 2 3 4 5 6 7 8 9 10
Bowel Disturbance (Diarrhea/ Constipation)	1 2 3 4 5 6 7 8 9 10
Breathing Difficulty	1 2 3 4 5 6 7 8 9 10
Choking Feeling	1 2 3 4 5 6 7 8 9 10
Burning or Itching Skin	1 2 3 4 5 6 7 8 9 10
Chest Pains	1 2 3 4 5 6 7 8 9 10
Chills	1 2 3 4 5 6 7 8 9 10
Compulsive Behaviors (pulling hair, biting fingernails)	1 2 3 4 5 6 7 8 9 10
Crying	1 2 3 4 5 6 7 8 9 10
Dizziness	1 2 3 4 5 6 7 8 9 10
Don't Like Being Touched	1 2 3 4 5 6 7 8 9 10
Dry Mouth	1 2 3 4 5 6 7 8 9 10
Excessive Sweating (Not due to heat)	1 2 3 4 5 6 7 8 9 10
Fainting Spells	1 2 3 4 5 6 7 8 9 10
Fatigue	1 2 3 4 5 6 7 8 9 10
Fear of Dying	1 2 3 4 5 6 7 8 9 10
Fear of Losing Control	1 2 3 4 5 6 7 8 9 10

PHYSICAL SENSATION	INTENSITY OF SENSATIONS
Flushes (Feeling Hot)	1 2 3 4 5 6 7 8 9 10
Headaches	1 2 3 4 5 6 7 8 9 10
Hearing Problems	1 2 3 4 5 6 7 8 9 10
High Blood Pressure	1 2 3 4 5 6 7 8 9 10
Incoordination	1 2 3 4 5 6 7 8 9 10
Lightheadedness	1 2 3 4 5 6 7 8 9 10
Muscle Tension	1 2 3 4 5 6 7 8 9 10
Muscle Tics	1 2 3 4 5 6 7 8 9 10
Muscles Spasms	1 2 3 4 5 6 7 8 9 10
Numbness	1 2 3 4 5 6 7 8 9 10
Palpitations (Heart pounding or fluttering)	1 2 3 4 5 6 7 8 9 10
Rapid Heart Beat	1 2 3 4 5 6 7 8 9 10
Skin Problems	1 2 3 4 5 6 7 8 9 10
Spaced Out feeling (like things are unreal)	1 2 3 4 5 6 7 8 9 10
Tingling	1 2 3 4 5 6 7 8 9 10
Hand Trembling	1 2 3 4 5 6 7 8 9 10
Unsteady walking or balance	1 2 3 4 5 6 7 8 9 10
Visual Disturbances	1 2 3 4 5 6 7 8 9 10
Vomiting	1 2 3 4 5 6 7 8 9 10
Clenching your teeth	1 2 3 4 5 6 7 8 9 10

Factor 3: Stressors

Below, in the left column, are a list of life stressors. If you have not experienced this stressor recently, do not circle any number in the right column. If you have experienced this stressor, circle a number from 1-10. The higher the number, the more intense the stressor has been (Ex. 1-

bothers me a little, 5-bothers me a moderate amount, 10-bothers me a great deal).

STRESSORS	INTENSITY OF STRESSORS
I have not been able to make up my mind about some issues that have remained unresolved for a long time (feeling in limbo)	1 2 3 4 5 6 7 8 9 10
I have experienced relationship problems with my romantic partner	1 2 3 4 5 6 7 8 9 10
I have experienced separation from my romantic partner	1 2 3 4 5 6 7 8 9 10
I was divorced from my romantic partner	1 2 3 4 5 6 7 8 9 10
My romantic partner was unfaithful to me	1 2 3 4 5 6 7 8 9 10
I have experienced relationship problems with my parents	1 2 3 4 5 6 7 8 9 10
I have experienced relationship problems with my children	1 2 3 4 5 6 7 8 9 10
I have experienced relationship problems with my siblings	1 2 3 4 5 6 7 8 9 10
I have experienced relationship problems with extended family	1 2 3 4 5 6 7 8 9 10
I have experienced relationship problems with my friends	1 2 3 4 5 6 7 8 9 10
I have experienced relationship problems with my neighbors	1 2 3 4 5 6 7 8 9 10
I have experienced relationship problems with my boss	1 2 3 4 5 6 7 8 9 10
I have experienced relationship problems with my coworkers	1 2 3 4 5 6 7 8 9 10
I entered school	1 2 3 4 5 6 7 8 9 10

STRESSORS	INTENSITY OF STRESSORS
I began puberty	1 2 3 4 5 6 7 8 9 10
I graduated from school	1 2 3 4 5 6 7 8 9 10
I started a new job or career	1 2 3 4 5 6 7 8 9 10
I became engaged to marry	1 2 3 4 5 6 7 8 9 10
I got married	1 2 3 4 5 6 7 8 9 10
I became a parent	1 2 3 4 5 6 7 8 9 10
My child left home	1 2 3 4 5 6 7 8 9 10
I started Menopause	1 2 3 4 5 6 7 8 9 10
I retired from work	1 2 3 4 5 6 7 8 9 10
I have had memory problems due to my age	1 2 3 4 5 6 7 8 9 10
I have taken care of a physically or mentally incapacitated person	1 2 3 4 5 6 7 8 9 10
I have experienced personal illness	1 2 3 4 5 6 7 8 9 10
I have been physically injured	1 2 3 4 5 6 7 8 9 10
I was in an accident	1 2 3 4 5 6 7 8 9 10
I underwent surgery	1 2 3 4 5 6 7 8 9 10
I had an abortion	1 2 3 4 5 6 7 8 9 10
A close family member has experienced personal illness	1 2 3 4 5 6 7 8 9 10
I have been fired or laid off from work	1 2 3 4 5 6 7 8 9 10
I have been chronically unemployed	1 2 3 4 5 6 7 8 9 10
I have had academic problems	1 2 3 4 5 6 7 8 9 10
I have experienced job dissatisfaction	1 2 3 4 5 6 7 8 9 10
I have experienced uncertainty about career choices	1 2 3 4 5 6 7 8 9 10

STRESSORS	INTENSITY OF STRESSORS
My living circumstances have changed (where I live)	1 2 3 4 5 6 7 8 9 10
I am concerned about personal safety in my neighborhood/ residence	1 2 3 4 5 6 7 8 9 10
I have had financial problems	1 2 3 4 5 6 7 8 9 10
I have been arrested	1 2 3 4 5 6 7 8 9 10
I have been imprisoned	1 2 3 4 5 6 7 8 9 10
I have been involved in a lawsuit	1 2 3 4 5 6 7 8 9 10
I have been on Trial	1 2 3 4 5 6 7 8 9 10
I have experienced verbal abuse by others	1 2 3 4 5 6 7 8 9 10
I have experienced physical abuse by others	1 2 3 4 5 6 7 8 9 10
I have experienced sexual abuse by others	1 2 3 4 5 6 7 8 9 10
I have moved from another country/culture to the United States	1 2 3 4 5 6 7 8 9 10
I have experienced uncertainty about my sexual orientation	1 2 3 4 5 6 7 8 9 10
I have experienced a Natural Disaster	1 2 3 4 5 6 7 8 9 10
I have experienced a Man-made Disaster	1 2 3 4 5 6 7 8 9 10
I have experienced Persecution	1 2 3 4 5 6 7 8 9 10
I have experienced an unwanted pregnancy	1 2 3 4 5 6 7 8 9 10
I was raped	1 2 3 4 5 6 7 8 9 10
I have experienced the death of a romantic partner	1 2 3 4 5 6 7 8 9 10
I have experienced the death of a close family member	1 2 3 4 5 6 7 8 9 10

STRESSORS	INTENSITY OF STRESSORS
I have experienced the death of a close friend	1 2 3 4 5 6 7 8 9 10

Factor 4: Negative Coping Style

Below, in the left column, are a list of negative coping styles. If you have engaged in a coping style that has hurt you either emotionally, physically, financially, or socially in recent months circle a number from 1-10. The higher the number, the more hurtful the coping style has been for you (Ex. 1-has hurt me somewhat, 5-has hurt me a moderate amount, 10-has hurt me a great deal).

NEGATIVE COPING STYLE	INTENSITY OF COPING STYLE (1-10)
Alcohol	1 2 3 4 5 6 7 8 9 10
Illicit Drugs	1 2 3 4 5 6 7 8 9 10
Prescription Drugs	1 2 3 4 5 6 7 8 9 10
Cigarette Smoking	1 2 3 4 5 6 7 8 9 10
Overeating	1 2 3 4 5 6 7 8 9 10
Undereating	1 2 3 4 5 6 7 8 9 10
Cleaning/Organizing	1 2 3 4 5 6 7 8 9 10
Sex	1 2 3 4 5 6 7 8 9 10
Sleeping	1 2 3 4 5 6 7 8 9 10
Gambling	1 2 3 4 5 6 7 8 9 10
Shopping/Spending	1 2 3 4 5 6 7 8 9 10
Working too much	1 2 3 4 5 6 7 8 9 10
Exercising too much	1 2 3 4 5 6 7 8 9 10
Acting impulsively too often	1 2 3 4 5 6 7 8 9 10
I don't like trying new things	1 2 3 4 5 6 7 8 9 10
Occasionally, I have cut myself purposely to "feel" something or distract myself	1 2 3 4 5 6 7 8 9 10

NEGATIVE COPING STYLE	INTENSITY OF COPING STYLE (1-10)
Being overly critical of others	1 2 3 4 5 6 7 8 9 10
Saying YES to others when I should say NO	1 2 3 4 5 6 7 8 9 10
Avoiding others too much	1 2 3 4 5 6 7 8 9 10
Being overly verbally aggressive	1 2 3 4 5 6 7 8 9 10
Being overly physically aggressive	1 2 3 4 5 6 7 8 9 10
Being too "clingy" with others	1 2 3 4 5 6 7 8 9 10
Blaming others for my own mistakes	1 2 3 4 5 6 7 8 9 10
Deliberately annoying others	1 2 3 4 5 6 7 8 9 10
Staying in an abusive relationship	1 2 3 4 5 6 7 8 9 10
Repeatedly lying to others	1 2 3 4 5 6 7 8 9 10
Dropping all of my friends when I get a new romantic partner	1 2 3 4 5 6 7 8 9 10
Not being a good listener	1 2 3 4 5 6 7 8 9 10
Not being well mannered	1 2 3 4 5 6 7 8 9 10
Not initiating conversations when I should	1 2 3 4 5 6 7 8 9 10
Having a lot of temper tantrums	1 2 3 4 5 6 7 8 9 10

Factor 5: Unfulfilled Needs

Below, in the left column, are a list of statements. If you agree with a statement, circle YES and if you disagree, circle NO. If you circle NO, this indicates that you may not be getting this human need fulfilled.

UNFULFILLED NEEDS	INTENSITY OF UNFULFILLED NEEDS (1-10)
Most of the time I have enough good food available to me.	YES NO

UNFULFILLED NEEDS	INTENSITY OF UNFULFILLED NEEDS (1-10)	
Most of the time, I have a place to live that is warm, shelters me from the elements, and is safe.	YES	NO
Most of the time, I am pain free.	YES	NO
Most of the time, I get enough sleep.	YES	NO
Most of the time, I get enough sexual release.	YES	NO
Most of the time, I urinate and defecate without problems.	YES	NO
I have at least one consistent relationship with another person where there is sharing, caring, empathy, concern, self disclosure, and give-and-take.	YES	NO
I communicate/socialize enough with others.	YES	NO
I am currently in a relationship with others (children, spouse, siblings, etc.) where I can provide nurturance and caring.	YES	NO
I have someone to talk to who will listen to me and understand "where I'm coming from."	YES	NO
I have enough opportunities to keep up with what others are doing (friends, neighbors, family, coworkers, celebrities, etc.).	YES	NO
I provide enough time for myself to relax.	YES	NO
I have enough stimulation in my life.	YES	NO
I have a good balance between "doing for myself" and "doing for others."	YES	NO
I have a good balance between "doing my own thing" and "conforming to societies values."	YES	NO

UNFULFILLED NEEDS	INTENSITY OF UNFULFILLED NEEDS (1-10)	
I have a sense of my identity or who I am. (Identity can be defined by one's **role** (mother, father, husband, wife, brother, sister, son, daughter), **religion** (Christian, Jew, etc.) **nationality** (American, Mexican, etc.) **heritage** (Irish, Italian, etc.) **job** (plumber, housewife, engineer, etc.), and **family background** (e.g., I'm a 4th generation McCoy originally from Ireland, etc.). **Traditions** and **rituals** also give people a sense of who they are.	YES	NO
I appreciate other people's creativity (art, architecture, music, photography, writing, poetry, stories, movies, TV, etc.) and/or produce my own works of creativity.	YES	NO
Generally, I feel that I have control over myself and my environment.	YES	NO

Section B: We Interact With the World Through our Senses

We interact with the world through our five senses. These senses are constantly being bombarded with stimuli from our environment. What we choose to expose our senses to will influence our happiness level.

"Action may not always bring happiness, but there is no happiness without action."

Benjamin Disraeli

Chapter # 8: How Music and Speech Change Your Mood

What we HEAR

We *HEAR* Music and it Affects Our Mood

- Music has been used by humans for thousands of years to induce a particular mood.

- Note how music is used at many ceremonies (weddings, funerals, graduations, etc.) to evoke a mood in the participants. It is used in movies and television to make the action more exciting or dramas more intense.

- Music can affect your mood in at least three different ways. First, the tempo, volume, and instrumentation can directly stimulate and/or relax you. Secondly, if you have a particular memory associated with a song, hearing that song again can evoke a similar mood to the one you experienced initially during that event. Finally, if the song has lyrics, the words can evoke emotions as well.

- You can (and probably do) use music as a means of stimulation or relaxation. You may have favorite music on a CD or portable music player, or listen to particular radio stations. Psychotherapist Carol Merle-Fishman in her book *The Music Within You*, suggests that you start out by matching your music to your current mood, and then gradually change the sound until it mirrors the mood you wish to experience. You can also try jumping directly into music which is the opposite of your current mood, and see if that can rapidly alter your mood.

- Try using music to change your current undesirable mood state. For instance, if you are anxious or uptight, try listening to more relaxing music. If you are feeling sad or lazy, try listening to more upbeat, stimulating music.

- To relax, you may want to listen to soft instrumental music such as light jazz, new age, or classical guitar. You can buy CDs or MP3s of music specifically recorded to be relaxing (some include soothing sounds of nature as well). Sounds of water (waves crashing, bubbles, gurgling, and rain) are often relaxing. Wind blowing in the trees or the sounds of crickets or frogs can also be relaxing.

- For stimulation, you may want to listen to rousing dance music, rock, classical or any other upbeat music of your choice.

We *HEAR* people talking to us, and us talking back to them.

- <u>Listening to someone else</u> - It is obvious that hearing someone's speech can affect us. (A rousing speech, an argument, etc.) The content and inflection of speech affect our mood. Your mood will certainly change depending upon whether you are listening to a positive, supportive person, or a critical, demeaning one.

- <u>Listening to ourselves</u> - Sometimes we are happy about things we've said to others and sometimes we feel negative about words that have come out of our mouth.

Chapter # 9: How to Use Light to Improve Your Mood

What we SEE

How Light May Affect Your Mood

- Some people are affected by the amount and intensity of light around them. Many people feel lethargic or low when the weather is consistently dark and cloudy for days at a time. As soon as a bright, sunny day appears, their mood usually improves. For certain people, a lack of bright light actually promotes clinical depression. As many as 15% of Americans who live in northern latitudes suffer from a mild form of seasonal affective disorder, which causes low moods and energy, especially in the winter. Treatment for low moods brought on by darkness includes exposure to bright artificial light in the early morning and late afternoon.

- You may want to observe your mood and see if it varies with the amount of light you are receiving. If it does, you may want to turn on more lights, use different lights (e.g., halogen lamps which produce more natural light), or try different tinted lights and see if it affects your mood.

- Different types of skylight may evoke a differential mood. Dawn, Bright daylight, Cloudiness, Dusk, or Night all may induce different mood states.

What we see with our eyes open (i.e., the real world)

- **People** - Who we see affects our mood (Friends, enemies, family members, attractive strangers, movie stars, etc.)

- **Places** (water, grass, trees and/or mountains, buildings, etc.) - Looking at a beautiful scene of nature or a slum certainly promotes different mood states.

- **Things** - This covers almost everything else. Personnel possessions, works of art, etc.

We also "see" with our eyes closed by visualizing images in our mind,

or imagery - by visualizing different actions, places, or events in your mind, you can affect your feelings, thoughts, and behaviors.

Imagery can help you:

- **Relax** (See Chapter # 38)
- Decrease pain
- Achieve your goals (By actually visualizing positive completion of each step of a process).

Color - Dark colors evoke a more somber mood while lighter pastels induce a more upbeat atmosphere.

Sights of Nature - Natural settings like beaches, mountains, green meadows, etc. can produce relaxing and positive mood states. These terrains usually include some of the following:

- Water
  - a. Lakes
  - b. Ponds
  - c. Ocean
- Plants
  - a. Trees
  - b. Bushes
  - c. Grass
  - d. Flowers
- Sky
  - a. Clouds
  - b. Stars
  - c. Blue sky
  - d. Mountains

Stories we see/hear - People usually perceive stories through hearing, seeing, or both. Any of the following certainly can affect our mood.

- Movies, TV, books, etc.

- Comedies, comedians, etc. which make us laugh. (See Chapter # 41)

Chapter # 10: What You Feel and Touch Can Affect Your Mood

What we FEEL/TOUCH

- The skin can perceive pressure, temperature, pain, wetness/dryness, and texture.

- Negative sensations like extreme cold, heat, humidity, or pain can promote a negative mood.

- Positive sensations can promote a positive mood (see the following):

  - Moderate temperature

  - Getting a massage

  - Moving the body (exercise, dancing, etc.)

  - Feeling a gentle breeze

  - Swimming, taking a hot bath, shower, or sauna. Thirty minutes in a sauna can reduce tension and may raise blood levels of endorphins (natural painkillers thought to produce feelings of well-being and euphoria) according to psychologists Robert Ornstein and David Sobel.

"Thousands of candles can be lighted from a single candle, and the life of the candle will not be shortened. Happiness never decreases by being shared."

Buddha

Chapter # 11: How Smelling Certain Aromas Can Affect Your Mood

What we SMELL

- The nose is very sensitive and can detect the scent of just a few stray molecules in the air. With more than 6 million smell receptor cells, our noses can distinguish 10,000 different smells.

- Smell is almost completely responsible for the sensation we call taste.

- Each person emits a genetically encoded "odor print" that is as distinctive as our fingerprints.

- Pheromones, specialized olfactory substances produced by most animal species, communicate sexual receptivity, territorial rights and social status in many animal species. They probably have some effect on human sexual response.

- Aromachology is the study of the powers of aroma. Some substances may have mood-altering capabilities. However, critics believe that the associative power of individual aromas reduces the likelihood of their having any universal effects. Nonetheless, most people like the following smells:

  ▸ Freshly cut grass

  ▸ Salty ocean air

  ▸ Flowers

  ▸ Food cooking

"Happiness is a thing to be practiced, like the violin."

John Lubbock

Chapter # 12: How Food Can Affect Your Mood

What we EAT/TASTE

Eating (See Chapter # 50) a healthy diet can promote your mental health. People require a certain amount of protein, carbohydrates, vitamins, minerals, and salts (i.e., a balanced diet) to feel good both physically and mentally. Deficiencies in any of these areas can lead to problems.

- It is probably better to get proper nutrition from diet alone. Nutritional supplements make many fantastic claims to improve health and energy, but their safety and efficacy are debatable to say the least.

How food can affect your mood

- Certain foods like candy bars which are loaded with simple sugars can briefly increase energy levels but they are short-lived, and as your insulin levels rise and blood sugar dips, you may experience irritability, sadness, or anxiety. Some people need to eat more frequently (snacks between meals) to maintain even blood sugar levels and stable mood.

- Some foods influence the production of brain chemicals that are directly involved in determining our mood, mental energy, performance and behavior (Judith Wurtman, nutrition researcher at MIT):

- **Water** - Drinking enough water each day can prevent you from feeling lethargic. Caffeinated soft drinks and coffee may not hydrate you as well as water because the caffeine can act as diuretic and increase dehydration.

- **Tyrosine** - Turkey, tuna or chicken (high in tyrosine) boosts levels of brain chemicals dopamine and norepinephrine, and in turn improves motivation and reaction time. U.S. Military research has indicated that tyrosine lifts energy levels and helps the body to cope better with stress.

- **Iron** - Keeps the body's cells fueled with oxygen.

- **Magnesium** - (magnesium-rich foods include bananas, nuts, beans, leafy greens, and wheat germ). Increases in Magnesium intake may reduce anxiety and improve sleep. Stress hormones (during times of stress) drain Magnesium from cells, resulting in lower resistance to colds, viruses and a tired feeling.

- **Calcium** - Foods rich in calcium, such as dairy products or beans, can help fight symptoms of depression according to Dr. Larry Christensen, Professor of Psychology at Texas A & M University.

- **Chocolate** - A favorite with many people; its taste and texture bring pleasure world-wide. It contains fat, sugar, caffeine, and other chemicals which may activate the pleasure centers of the brain. If you love it as many do, try to eat it in moderation.

Section C: Techniques To Help You Learn New Behaviors, Avoid Old Behaviors, and Face Your Fears

"Happiness is not in having or being
- it is in the doing."

Lillian Watson

Chapter # 13: Stimulus Control

Stimulus Control - the presence of certain stimuli tends to increase the frequency of certain behaviors.

<u>Removing stimuli to decrease behaviors.</u>

Example: The sight of chocolate cake (the stimulus) may increase the likelihood that you will eat the cake (eating behavior). If you're trying to lose weight, the stimulus, chocolate cake, should be kept out of sight. Therefore, you control the stimulus by not buying chocolate cake, and keeping it out of the house.

<u>Including stimuli to increase behaviors.</u>

Example: Let's say you exercise better when listening to the stimulus, "music." By including music in your workout (i.e., controlling the stimulus) you are increasing desirable behaviors (i.e., exercise).

"Happiness is the full use of your powers along lines of excellence."

John F. Kennedy

Chapter # 14: Modeling

Modeling - observing other's behaviors and copying that behavior. This is how children and chimps learn; by emulating their caregivers. Adults, of course, use this method of learning as well.

> **Example**: Let's say you are trying to become a good public speaker. You watch videos of great public speakers and try to **model** some of their facial expressions, voice, and gestures.

"Happiness is an expression of the soul in considered actions."

Aristotle

Chapter # 15: Behavioral Rehearsal or Role-Playing

Behavioral Rehearsal (Role-playing) - practicing new behaviors or thoughts repeatedly until they become more natural.

Just like an actor practicing for a role, you can rehearse your "lines" until you know them cold. It may be helpful to have another person to practice with or audio/video tape yourself to obtain objective feedback about your performance.

> **Example**: You can practice being assertive (See Chapter 21) with a friend before actually trying out your assertiveness skills with a "real" person.

> **Example**: You want to ask your boss for a raise, but you are nervous about it. By rehearsing your "speech" with someone else, you can decide what to say and lower your anxiety level.

"The happiness that is genuinely satisfying is accompanied by the fullest exercise of our faculties and the fullest realization of the world in which we live."

Bertrand Russell

Chapter # 16: Reward Yourself and Others For Positive Behaviors

■ Reward behaviors you wish to encourage.

■ The reward can be tangible objects (e.g., food or money) or time at a favorite activity.

■ Reward yourself when you do something beneficial for yourself, and reward others when they do something you like.

■ Rewarding others can be something simple like a heart-felt "Thank You," or some other token of appreciation.

Example: You set a goal for yourself (e.g., throw out a bunch of old bills and papers), completed the goal, and rewarded yourself by downloading some MP3s of your favorite band.

Example: Your child just completed a chore without having to ask him (e.g., taking out the garbage). You thank him and give him a hug as a way to reward him and encourage future positive behaviors.

"Growth itself contains the germ of happiness."

Pearl S. Buck

Chapter # 17: Systematic Exposure

Systematic Exposure - consists basically of slowly, step-by-step, exposing yourself to feared situations. You gradually increase the frequency or intensity until you are able to face the feared situation fully. The more exposure to the feared situation, the less fearful you will become.

You can use other techniques to "prep" yourself for exposure like **modeling** (view how do others do it), **positive imagery** (using your mind to project positive outcomes) or **relaxation** (reducing anticipatory anxiety).

> **Example**: If you are afraid of spiders, you can first read about spiders, then look at pictures of spiders, and finally go to the zoo to see a real spider. Over time you will realize that your overreaction is more than is warranted (Black Widows excepted of course!).

"The happiest moments of my life have been the few which I have passed at home in the bosom of my family."

Thomas Jefferson

Section D: Social Interaction

"Let us be grateful to people who make us happy; they are the charming gardeners who make our souls blossom."

Marcel Proust

Chapter # 18: Increase Amount of Meaningful Social Contact

Interpersonal relationships are very important to our happiness, survival, and personality development. Research indicates that a person's "perception" of social support is more important than actual support. In other words, you can be surrounded by many people or acquaintances (quantity) and still feel alone or unsupported. Conversely, in some cases, having one close relationship can provide you with all the social support you need.

Benefits of Social Support

- Social relationships help people to survive and propagate.

- They often provide the most pleasure and pain we derive out of life.

- They help us cope better with **stressors** (See Chapter # 4 for a complete list of stressors) (e.g., illness, job loss, etc.)

"Whoever is happy will make others happy, too."

Mark Twain

Chapter # 19: Realities of Interacting With Others

No one can change another person. You can <u>only</u> change yourself. If you are dissatisfied with an interpersonal relationship you have three options:

- Change the way you *think* about the other person; **Accept** (See Chapter # 23) the person as he/she is (or certain aspects of that person's behavior/values).

- Change the way you *interact* with the person. Interaction includes **Communications Skills** (See Chapter # 20) and **Assertiveness Skills** (See Chapter # 21).

- **End your relationship** with that person. (See Chapter # 22).

"Love is the master key which opens the gates of happiness."
Oliver Wendell Holmes

Chapter # 20: Communication Skills

Here are some suggestions to improve your relationships with others (family, friends, coworkers, etc.) These ideas should help you begin and maintain positive relationships.

LISTEN - Very few people do this well. When others talk, really pay attention to what they are saying. Try to understand their point of view and their feelings. Acknowledge that you're listening both verbally (say uh huh, yeah, etc.) and non-verbally (nod your head, eye contact). If you're listening well, you should be able to restate in your own words, the essence of the other person's communication. Avoid interrupting the person as they speak.

SPEAKING TO OTHERS - When speaking to others it is generally appropriate to establish regular eye contact, speak loud enough to be heard, speak clearly, and have an interested facial expression.

Who would you rather listen to?

- Someone who looks you in the eye, exhibits good posture, speaks loud enough to be heard, speaks clearly, in terms which you understand, has an interested facial expression, who has honorable intentions, and who tries to understand your point of view.

OR

- Someone who doesn't look at you when speaking, slouches, looks bored, mumbles, rambles, is manipulative, and thinks his point of view is the only right point of view.

COMPROMISE - When trying to resolve a dispute, both parties must give a little, and get a little. Entertain the possibility that you could be wrong! Try to see the other person's point of view. Try to make it a win-win situation rather than win-lose one.

INTEREST - Become genuinely interested in other people's lives. Ask them about their day, their interests, their life.

APPRECIATION - Give honest and sincere appreciation verbally (e.g., thank you), or perhaps a thoughtful gesture (e.g., a card), etc.

HONESTY - In general, try to be honest with others (white lies are appropriate on occasion).

HUMOR - Try not to take yourself too seriously.

MANNERS -

- Be Respectful (e.g., don't talk down to others or call them names; treat them as the fellow human beings they are).

- Be Considerate (e.g., clean up after yourself).

- Be Polite (e.g., say please, thank you, etc.).

REQUESTS - In general, if you ask others to do something rather than telling them to do it, they will respond with less resentment or rebelliousness. It's even better if you can ask their opinion about how something should be done.

RESPONSIBILITY - In general, do what you say you are going to do (unless there are extenuating circumstance, of course) (e.g., show up on time, call if you can't make an appointment, etc.)

FEEDBACK - Give others positive as well as negative feedback. People want to know what they are doing right, as well as what they're doing wrong. When giving criticism, do it gently, make it specific and make it clear that you are criticizing a specific behavior, not the person.

NOBODY'S PERFECT - Don't expect perfection from yourself or others, or you will be disappointed. We all make mistakes.

CHANGE - You cannot change other people. The only one you can change is yourself.

BOUNDARIES - All people are entitled to some privacy (thoughts, personal space) and time to be alone.

APOLOGIZE - If you make a mistake, say you're sorry.

Chapter # 21: How to Appropriately Assert Your Rights, Share Your Thoughts and Feelings

Appropriate assertive behavior consists of standing up for your personal rights and expressing your thoughts, feelings, and beliefs in direct, honest, and appropriate way without violating other people's rights. This includes 4 specific response patterns:

- The ability to say NO
- The ability to ask for favors or to make requests
- The ability to express positive or negative feelings (love, appreciation, affection, and anger)
- The ability to initiate, continue and terminate conversations.

A Non-Assertive person will:

- Rarely express their thoughts or feelings.
- Go along with what others want to do much of the time at the expense of their own wishes.
- Superficially agree with others, and then covertly do exactly what they want to do anyway.
- Have great difficulty saying no.
- Hesitate to initiate conversations.
- Agree with others so they will like them.

Assertiveness is a skill based on the idea that your needs, wants, and feelings are neither more nor less important than those of other people; they are equally important. You should, therefore, make claims for yourself appropriately, honestly, and clearly. Learning how to do this helps ensure that you do not come away from situations feeling bad about yourself, or leaving others feeling bad.

Assertiveness as a compromise - Assertiveness skills can be seen as the happy medium between extremes:

The extremes of aggression and passivity do not work well most of the time.

- Passive approach - Taking a passive approach will either result in not getting your needs met at all (i.e., not asking for things or sharing your thoughts) or becoming "passive-aggressive" (i.e., trying to get your needs met in a covert or indirect way).

- Aggressive approach - The aggressive approach can involve talking over others, not listening to others, or not taking other's feelings into consideration. Most people do not like those individuals who are aggressive.

The extremes of caring only for yourself or only for others. Assertiveness is not being selfish (caring only for yourself) or completely sacrificing your own needs for others. It is a compromise.

Ideally one should be able to: lead their life the way they want to, believe what they want, and express their thoughts and feelings in an appropriate fashion. Unfortunately, in many countries people do not have such freedoms.

Benefits of Assertiveness:

- Gaining the respect of others
- Reduction of angry feelings toward others
- Improved self-esteem
- Getting your needs met

What Assertiveness Will **Not** Do

- It will not necessarily guarantee you happiness or fair treatment by others, nor will it solve all your personal problems or guarantee that others will be assertive and not aggressive with you.

- Just because you assert yourself does not mean you will always get what you want.

Specific Techniques for Assertiveness

- Be as specific and clear as possible about what you want, think, and feel.

- Be direct. Deliver your message to the person for whom it is intended, not outsiders.

- Acknowledge that your message comes from your frame of reference. You can acknowledge ownership with personalized ("I") statements such as "I don't agree with you" (as compared to "You're wrong") or "I'd like you to mow the lawn" (as compared to "You really should mow the lawn, you know").

- Ask for feedback. "Am I being clear? How do you see this situation? What do you want to do?" Asking for feedback can encourage others to correct any misperceptions you may have as well as help others realize that you are expressing an opinion, feeling, or desire rather than a demand.

"Happiness is not a destination. It is a method of life."

Burton Hills

Chapter # 22: Ending Relationships

There are appropriate times to end relationships with others (e.g., constant verbal, physical, or sexual abuse) or when you decide that you cannot accept certain behaviors of others. You may ask, "How do I bail out? I can't bring myself to leave or I've tried to leave before and keep going back." Leaving someone is often easier said than done. There are many reasons why people have difficulty leaving relationships when they know (intellectually, at least) that the relationship is bad for them and does not promise to improve. Here are some reasons:

■ You are afraid of being alone and/or doubt you will find someone else.

■ You are afraid of physical or verbal abuse/retaliation from the person you are leaving.

■ You don't think very highly of yourself and feel that you "deserve" to be treated poorly (This could be a conscious or unconscious belief).

■ You experience feelings of guilt at the thought of leaving the person.

■ You are worried about hurting the other person's feelings.

■ You keep thinking the other person will change and/or that you can change them.

■ You partially "enjoy" the chaos (ups and downs) the relationship brings.

■ You are worried about the financial repercussions of leaving this person.

■ You are worried how others will be affected by leaving the person (e.g., how will children be affected by leaving a husband or wife).

■ You enjoy the "good" parts of the relationship so much that you are willing to put up with the "bad" parts.

Here are some suggestions for leaving:

■ Build up outside sources of social support (i.e., friends, relatives, supports groups, etc.). It is very difficult to leave someone who is your sole source of emotional support.

■ Try new **activities** (See Chapter # 32) (hobbies, volunteering, classes, etc.) which make you feel good about yourself. Building up your **self-**

esteem (See Chapter # 58) may make it easier to separate because you may feel that you deserve to be treated better.

- Write a list of benefits and drawbacks of the relationship. Seeing them all on paper may have more impact than just thinking of them.

- Try to "emotionally separate" yourself from the person. By distancing yourself either physically and/or emotionally, you may feel less attached to that person and it may be easier to leave. (Don't be surprised if the person you are trying to leave attempts to "pull you back in").

- Try to refute irrational beliefs. For example, you will not die from being temporarily alone (you may even like it) and there is a chance you will meet someone who will treat you with respect and kindness.

- Try to deal with feelings of guilt by realizing that staying in this relationship will be negative for both you and the other person. If you stay in the relationship, chances are you will not be happy, and if you are not happy, the other person will probably not be happy either.

- Realize that you are getting some desirable things out of the relationship, but no matter how good they are, they are not worth the harmful ones.

Section E: More Positive Techniques to Change Your Thinking and Behaviors

"It isn't what you have, or who you are, or where you are, or what you are doing that makes you happy or unhappy. It is what you think about."
Dale Carnegie

Chapter # 23: Acceptance of Unchangeable Situations

Learn to differentiate between the things in life you have control over and those you don't; Accept the things you cannot change, and change the things you can. This is a paraphrase of the serenity prayer attributed to theologian Reinhold Niebuhr. Of course, this is easier said than done. What's done is done, and cannot be undone. As much as we might want to berate ourselves over past mistakes, choices, relationships, etc., the past is truly unchangeable. All we can do about the past is learn from our experiences and move on.

Remember

You made the best decisions you could at the time (to meet your needs or deal with stress). You cannot go back and change the past. You can currently identify other, better ways of getting your needs met. Acceptance can be a process that takes time and involves going through a series of emotions or it can come relatively quickly. Regardless of how long it takes, the goal is the same; Acceptance of unchangeable situations can reduce a lot of potential turmoil in your life.

"Happiness is a function of accepting what is."

Werner Erhard

Chapter # 24: Who You Compare Yourself to Affects How You Feel About Yourself

"How bitter a thing it is to look into happiness through another man's eyes" - **William Shakespeare**

Your level of happiness can be affected by whom you compare yourself to.

Helpful hint: Change who you compare yourself to. If you are constantly comparing yourself to people who are smarter, better looking, more successful, etc., you are setting yourself up for feeling negatively and possibly envious. The effects of Television shows like "Lifestyles of the Rich and Famous" present a skewed world of rich, beautiful people who are not representative of the public at large. If on the other hand you compare yourself with those who are less fortunate, you probably will feel grateful and fortunate.

Happiness is "an agreeable sensation arising from contemplating the misery of another" - **Ambrose Bierce, The Devils Dictionary.**

This may sound rather harsh, but it is true. It does not mean that you should constantly dwell on others less fortunate, but doing it once in a while may make you feel better. (See Chapter # 26 on **Counting your Blessings**).

One example of using this technique follows:

> Let's say the water pipes in your house /apartment broke and you can't get water for several hours. Instead of bemoaning your fate, you could think of the hundreds of millions of people in the world today who have no clean running water at any time.

Also, try and compare your life of democracy, freedom of choice and speech to most of the other people in the world today, and in the past. Does your life seem better?

Quite often, people compare themselves to those they live near or work with. For instance, if a person makes $50,000 per year and lives in a neighborhood where the average salary is $20,000, he/she may feel more fortunate than others. On the other hand, if the same person making $50,000 lives among others making $500,000 per year, he/she may feel deprived.

Misery loves company. When experiencing pain, failure, or other negative events, it can make us feel better to know that others are experiencing the same or worse discomfort. This is one reason group therapy is helpful to people. If you are having problems, chances are you don't want to hear how well everyone else is doing.

Another part of human nature is that people get used to, or adapt to, good things. There is an initial "high" associated with a new car, house, etc., but eventually you get used to the new "thing," and the thrill fades. This is why the rich are not much happier than middle class people; you get used to all the "goodies" money can buy and end up as happy as you were before. Nico Frijda, the Dutch emotion researcher said it well, *"continued pleasures wear off... Pleasure is always contingent upon change and disappears with continuous satisfaction. When you are truly hungry, food tastes great. When you are truly tired, sleep is the best. When you are lonely, meeting with others is a relief."*

Pleasure is also linked to pain. Sometimes, the ending of pain is pleasurable. Have you ever been sick, and then gotten better? The absence of discomfort or just feeling normal feels great compared to being sick.

Chapter # 25: Focus on the Present Rather than Waiting for a Happy Future

To maximize your happy times, it behooves you to savor every moment and detail that life has to offer *right now*. The Latin expression "Carpe Diem" which translates into "seize the moment" illustrates this point. Do things everyday that bring you happiness. Don't live all year for that one week of vacation. Enjoy the *process* and the *product* of your efforts, not just the *product*; especially since most of your time is spent on the process.

If you don't try to maximize your current level of happiness, you may do some of the following:

- Rehash old hurts, bitterness, and negative things from your past.

- Live in the successes and glories of "the good old days."

- Dream about the idealized day when your, "ship comes in." (Tomorrow may never arrive; If you believe you will finally be happy when you **buy** (See Chapter # 60) that new house, car or boat, you may be disappointed).

- Fret in worried anticipation about future events. Most of our **worries** (See Chapter # 52) never come true.

Of course, this does not mean that you should live totally in the present. One can learn from their past and should plan for their future, but focusing too much on the past or future can rob you of enjoyment in the present.

If you feel there is nothing presently to be happy about, try counting your **blessings** (See Chapter # 26) or **comparing** (See Chapter # 24) yourself to others less fortunate, or try some new **activities** (See Chapter # 32).

"Happiness is not something you postpone for the future; it is something you design for the present."

Jim Rohn

Chapter # 26: Count Your Blessings - Many People Don't Appreciate What They Already Have

Count your blessings (appreciate what you already have). This may sound trite, but it is true. Most people take things for granted. This may just be a function of human nature (i.e., never satisfied with the status quo, and striving for more than we have). Nevertheless, if we concentrate more on what we don't have rather than what we do have, we may be disappointed. (See information on your **expectations** (Chapter # 27) and **comparing** (Chapter # 24) yourself to others).

For instance, if you live in the United States you probably have:

- Freedom
- Human rights
- Plentiful and healthy food
- The ability to live where you want
- The ability to work where you want
- The ability to vote for whom you want

Most people take these advantages for granted, as if all people enjoy such freedoms. In fact, many people in the world live under dictatorships and don't have these freedoms.

Helpful Suggestions:

- Make a list of all your blessings. They will be many, I'm sure, and will probably outweigh your misfortunes.

- Don't focus on what you don't have; enjoy and delight in what you do have.

- As Ben Franklin said, *"Happiness is produced not so much by great pieces of good fortune that seldom happen as by little advantages that occur everyday."* In other words, happy people find pleasure in life's simple things (sunshine, blue sky, water, nature, music, play, conversation, reading, family, etc.)

"Man is fond of counting his troubles, but he does not count his joys. If he counted them up as he ought to, he would see that every lot has enough happiness provided for it.
Fyodor Dostoevsky

Chapter # 27: Maintaining Realistic Expectations of Yourself and Others

"BLESSED IS HE WHO EXPECTS NOTHING, FOR HE SHALL NEVER BE DISAPPOINTED" - ALEXANDER POPE, 1727 LETTER

This saying may be a little too pessimistic, but there is some truth to it. If your expectations always exceed your accomplishments; or if you always expect others to behave appropriately, then you will certainly be disappointed, angry, etc. Either extreme of optimism (Pollyanna) or pessimism is not healthy. You need a balance of optimism and realism. You must realize your own limitations, yet strive for personal excellence.

Let's briefly state what you can count on in this world:

- Gravity

- Life - you're reading this right now, so you are alive

- Death - it will happen eventually

- The sun rising and setting, (at least for the next few billion years)

- Growing older (if you don't die young)

- Change (nothing lasts forever. That includes good feelings, bad feelings, living situations, etc. *Remember,* Expect change)

- For some people, God

- Special friends, family, or spouses

- Stressful life events (See Chapter # 04)

Here are some other Expectations to consider:

- Don't expect to be happy every minute of every day. Mood fluctuates as a function of circumstances, hormones, hunger, etc.

- Don't expect perfection from yourself or others. This will only lead to disappointment. Of course, this does not mean that you cannot strive for excellence; just don't expect perfection.

- Some people will treat you badly regardless of how you treat them. A rabbi named Kushner illustrated this point with the humorous saying, "expecting the world to treat you fairly because you are a good person, is like expecting the bull not to attack you because you're a vegetarian."

- Life is not fair (Some people feel there is ultimate divine justice, others do not. It is matter of individual preference).

- Risk is inherent in living

- Assess your expectations of life. Are they realistic? If you get the things that you expect or want, will you then be truly happy?

Do you have false expectations like the following:

- Everyone should love me

- No one should reject me

- I have to be successful at everything I do

- I have to make a lot of money to be happy

- I should be perfect (i.e., not make mistakes)

- I should always get what I want

- Life should be without pain and require no effort

What should your expectations for life be? Here are some suggestions:

- I want to enjoy close, intimate **relationships** (See Chapter # 18) with other people

- I want to enjoy **work** (See Chapter # 59) that is challenging and meaningful

- I want to know **who I really am** (See Chapter # 45) and what my real **feelings** (See Chapter # 06) are (not what others think I should feel)

- I want to fulfill my basic human **needs** (See Chapter # 03) in a healthy way

- When you experience strong emotions (e.g., disappointment, anger, sadness) ask yourself what are the underlying expectations behind those emotions. Many times your expectations (and resulting feelings) will be justified; other times, your expectations may be unrealistic or wrong. This does not mean that you should deny your inner feelings.

However, it can be helpful to know what your underlying expectations are, so if you choose, in the future, you can alter erroneous expectations.

- Be flexible! Life never goes 100% according to plan.

- When learning a new skill, don't expect to become an expert instantaneously. Make your goals short-term, achievable, and realistic to avoid disappointment.

"We tend to forget that happiness doesn't come as a result of getting something we don't have, but rather of recognizing and appreciating what we do have."

Frederick Keonig

Chapter # 28: Ways to Acquire a Positive Outlook on Life

Why do some people who have none of life's "good things," still manage to be joyfully happy, and others, who possess all the blessings of life, come up dissatisfied and unfulfilled? The reason is attitude. No matter how much success you have gained or possessions you have accumulated, happiness is largely contingent on whether you see your life as "half-full" or "half-empty." Generally, optimistic people, no matter how bad their situation, look on the bright side of life and end-up genuinely happy. Pessimistic people, no matter how well life treats them, look on the dark side, and are never content.

Sometimes, it is the way we interpret events, rather than the events themselves that affect our mood.

> For example, two families have their houses destroyed by tornadoes. Subsequently, one family may bemoan their fate, and ask themselves, "Oh, why me?" and dwell on the negative. The other family would be grateful for their lives being spared, rejoice in the help they receive from others, etc. Both families experienced identical events, but one family is miserable and the other optimistic. The only difference is attitude. A related component is **acceptance** (See Chapter #23). Most likely, the optimistic family has accepted what has happened. The other family is unaccepting, bitter, and miserable.

Also, note that:

- Happiness is a feeling that occurs in your mind; it doesn't occur in the outside world of events and people.

- When bad or negative things do happen, try to see the good or positive aspects of them, count your **blessings** (See Chapter # 26), and **compare** (See Chapter # 24) yourself with others. Remember, this does not mean you should put on a perennial happy face. It is O.K. and normal to experience negative emotions. Moreover, having realistic **expectations** (See Chapter # 27) can diminish the intensity and/or length of the negative emotions.

How to be more optimistic

- Practice looking on the bright side of events, the positive aspects of other people, and the special qualities you posses.

- Make a list of all the positive things you have going for you, and reflect upon those several times a day.

- Check your thinking periodically throughout the day. Try setting an alarm or write yourself little notes to check your thinking. When you get these little reminders, consider what you've been thinking about. If it's negative, **STOP the thought** (See Chapter # 44) and shift your attention to a more pleasant one. The more pleasant thoughts you have throughout the day, the happier you will be.

Chapter # 29: For Some People, Spirituality Can Fulfill Many Needs

For some people, religious faith or spirituality can increase happiness, and help them deal with stress. This is especially true if one views their "higher power" as warm, caring, and dependable rather than punitive, vengeful, unresponsive or rigid.

Spirituality fulfills a number of human needs:

- It can give a person a sense of identity (e.g., I am a Jew, Christian, Muslim, etc.).

- It can give **meaning** (See Chapter # 46) to one's life.

- It can lessen the anxiety of death (i.e., belief in an afterlife).

- It can give people more perceived control of their lives (prayer).

- It can give structure to people's lives (rituals, traditions, hierarchy).

- It can give people the feeling of ultimate acceptance.

- Finally, it can provide social contact and support (e.g., attending religious services).

Research indicates that religiously active people are less likely to abuse drugs, be divorced, commit suicide, and are more likely to be physically healthier & live longer. These findings can be interpreted in several ways.

- Some believe prayer gets direct results

- Religious prohibitions against alcohol, suicide, and divorce lessen the occurrence of these phenomena.

- Religious people avoid unhealthy practices more than non-religious people (i.e., smoking, drinking, etc.)

- Because of the many human needs it fulfills (see above) spiritual people feel more in control of their lives which lowers their levels of anxiety and stress, with concomitant improvement in their health.

Note: This is not an endorsement for religiosity. It merely substantiates what some people find. Beliefs whether religious or not (i.e., thoughts) can affect the way a person feels. Whether these beliefs are ultimately true is probably inconsequential.

"Man needs, for his happiness, not only the enjoyment of this or that, but hope and enterprise and change."
Bertrand Russell

Chapter # 30: What Causes People to Behave as They Do

As an adult, your current **B**ehaviors, **T**houghts, and **F**eelings (BTF) emanate from two sources (genes and environment):

- <u>Your genes (from both your biological parents)</u>. These genes help determine both general and specific human nature. By general nature, I mean the needs all humans have (e.g., food, shelter, companionship, sex, etc.). By specific human nature, I am referring to individual temperament or personality characteristics (e.g., some people are naturally more extroverted than others). As an embryo develops, the mother's hormones, nutrition, overall health, and chemical intake (e.g., caffeine, alcohol, nicotine) also affect development of her unborn child.

After a child is born, he/she continues to grow and develop as does the brain. Genetic predisposition, though, only accounts for about 50% of an adult's current BTF's. The other 50% is due to environment.

- <u>Your past/current environment</u>. From birth, an infant is exposed to human beings (from individuals to groups to society at large). Our experiences with these humans actually change our brain chemistry and neural pathways and affect our BTF both as children and later as adults. Moreover, many of these early experiences are not remembered by the older child or adult. Nevertheless, these early experiences affect our BTF both as children and adults. Some refer to this phenomenon as our unconscious.

Small children have certain developmental needs, as mentioned above (to be held, fed, nurtured, listened to, etc.). Fulfillment of these needs by a caregiver will contribute to "normal development."

- When these needs are <u>not</u> fulfilled, (i.e., **neglect** - the parent is not doing something he/she is supposed to be doing) it can lead to a variety of circumstances:

  - The child/adult feeling there is *something wrong with them* since their parents did not fulfill these needs.

  - The child/adult feeling *angry or resentful* that these needs were not met.

  - The child/adult attempting to get these needs met *through other means* (acting out behaviors like stealing, getting in fights, tantrums, withdrawing, illness, etc.).

- <u>Parents overt behavior can lead to abnormal development of their children</u> (i.e., verbal, physical, or sexual abuse). **Abuse** can lead to the following circumstances:

  ▸ Feeling something is wrong with you, feeling angry and resentful, or trying to get needs met through other means (See above).

  ▸ A lack of trust towards others.

  ▸ An inability to feel different emotions (i.e., the child "numbs out" to avoid intense negative feelings).

  ▸ Experiencing frequent anxiety or depression.

  ▸ Feeling a lack of control over their circumstances and self.

- Parents who <u>fail to validate their children's feelings</u> by telling them what they <u>should</u>, and <u>should not</u> feel or <u>squelching any expression of feeling</u> by their children (e.g., be a man, don't cry!) can result in:

  ▸ Adults who don't know how they really feel.

  ▸ Adults unable to tolerate strong feelings.

  ▸ Resentment towards their parents.

- Parents who are critical, fault-finding, or expect perfection from their children may result in a child/adult who:

  ▸ Is never satisfied with his/her performance.

  ▸ Is self-critical.

  ▸ Is a people-pleaser who is constantly striving to receive praise and validation.

- Parents who are inconsistent (e.g., punishing one time for a behavior and not punishing the next time) can lead to children:

  ▸ Not knowing what to expect from their environment.

  ▸ Experiencing anxiety.

- As a child develops, the parent lets the child become more independent (explore on his own, go out with friends, make his own decisions, etc.). When a parent does not let the child gradually become more independent, a child/adolescent can become anxious when faced with going out on his own and/or resent the parent for not allowing greater independence.

■ Children exposed to "dysfunctional" families have probably:

▸ Learned (i.e., modeled) to do "dysfunctional things" consciously or unconsciously from their parents, peers, or friends.

▸ Reacted to the dysfunctional behavior of their parents, siblings, or friends in a way that was adaptive for them at the time (e.g., Acting out to get attention, Running away to avoid mistreatment, etc.); but this behavior is no longer adaptive for the adult.

▸ Developed ways to cope with internal negative feelings to help reduce the pain (drugs, alcohol, anorexia, obesity, etc.).

▸ Not learned functional behaviors (e.g., social skills) that one should have learned in the first place.

■ As an adult, you may still continue to act the same way you did when you were a child, even though this is no longer functional or appropriate behavior, and you may still expect others to react to you as your parents did.

■ Finally, experiences as an adult can affect your current BTFs. These include brain dysfunction due to short or long term exposure to harmful drugs, virus, accident, tumor, disease, hormonal imbalance, lack of oxygen to the brain, or stroke. On a more positive note, positive experiences (caring relationships with others, learning new coping skills and behaviors, etc.) can alter our current brain chemistry and change our BTFs for the better.

"The art of being happy lies in the power of extracting happiness from common things."

Henry Ward Beecher

Chapter # 31: Positive Statements to Repeat to Yourself Everyday

Some children in this world have been told repeatedly by their parents (or other care-givers) that they are lazy, stupid, can't do anything right, or that they should *never* have been born, etc. In addition, they may have been physically abused, which further solidified how worthless they felt about themselves. These children, in effect, learn from their parents that they are "no good." They have heard these negative messages over and over again. After a while, these parents don't have to repeat these negative statements; the child (and eventually the adult) consciously and unconsciously repeats them to him/herself (i.e., internalizes these statements). One way to counteract these internalized negative messages is to replace them with positive, self-affirming ones, *over and over again.*

The following are a list of positive statements that you can repeat to yourself everyday (either silently or out loud). At first these statements may just feel like empty words, but eventually, after hundreds of repetitions, they will feel more real, and you will internalize them. Remember, when repeating them, concentrate on their meaning and try to experience them as your own. Feel free to come up with your own Positive Affirmations as well.

- I don't have to be liked by everyone.

- I can make mistakes and still be O.K.

- I am a worthy person because I am human.

- I can only change myself.

- I will **accept** the things I cannot change (See Chapter # 23).

- I will have positive, intimate **relationships** with other people (See Chapters # 18-22).

- I can control some important areas of my life.

- I have much to be **thankful** for (See Chapter # 26).

- I deserve to have my **needs** fulfilled (See Chapter # 03).

- I like myself.

- My problems will not last forever.

- I am capable and confident.

- I will trust my **feelings** (See Chapter # 06).

- I can count on myself.

- I will accomplish my **goals**, slowly, and step by step (See Chapter # 47).

- I will be **organized** (See Chapter # 39).

- I will have **positive**, optimistic thoughts (See Chapter # 28).

- I will savor **today** (See Chapter # 25).

Chapter # 32: Leisure Activities, Hobbies, Etc. To Improve Your Enjoyment of Life

Trying out new activities can have many benefits including meeting new people, combating boredom, etc. Below is a list of such activities which may give you some ideas. Also, you may want to fill out Appendix # 3 which will help you list all the activities you currently enjoy; activities you've done in the past, but no longer do; and activities you would like to try in the future.

ACTION AND ADVENTURE - bungee jumping, canoeing, flying a plane, gambling, hang gliding, horror movies, hot air ballooning, kayaking, motorcycling, paragliding, rock climbing, roller coasters, skiing, skydiving, snow boarding, snowmobile, video games.

ASSEMBLY, MAINTENANCE, REPAIR, AND/OR RESTORATION - home (entire structure, or patios, pools, walls, gardens, etc.), auto, boat, plane.

ATTENDING CLUB, SOCIETY, OR ORGANIZATION MEETINGS - conservation, consumer, cultural/ethnic, discussion groups, feminist, fraternal, historical, hobby groups, military, neighborhood associations, political, professional, religious (going to church, synagogue, mosque, etc.), scouting, senior citizens groups, singles clubs, union, volunteer.

COLLECTING THINGS - antiques, autographs, bottles, cars, china, clocks, coins, comics, dolls, magazines, patches, shells, sports cards, stamps, toys.

COMPUTERS - blogging, data base, desktop publishing, e-mail, games, home budget, music, on-line services and/or internet, programming, word processing.

GAMES TO PLAY - air hockey, backgammon, billiards, board games, card games, card tricks, checkers, chess, darts, erector set, jacks, juggling, legos, magic, marbles, miniature golf, monopoly, nerf, parlor or word games, pinball, pool, puzzles (crossword), video games, yo-yo.

JOIN A GROUP - support or self-help groups - group therapy for various emotional problems (anxiety, substance/alcohol abuse, bereavement, depression, physical illnesses, obesity, etc.)

MONEY - investment, merchandising, money management (stocks, buying and selling), retirement planning, selling.

PLANTS AND ANIMALS - aquarium, bird watching, bonsai, flower arrangement, gardening, horticulture, landscaping, lecture guide at a museum or park, nature study; playing with, owning and/or showing animals (dogs, cats, birds), plant care, ponds, raising pigeons, whale watching, zoo.

TAKING A CLASS - (Adult Education, college, technical, correspondence courses, etc.) in: American Indian studies, art appreciation, biology, business management, computers, criminology, current affairs, ethnic studies, film, foreign language, geography, government, history, law, literature, math, medicine, music appreciation, mythology, navigation, office skills, philosophy, prehistoric animals, science, etc.

SPORTS - archery, backpacking, badminton, baseball, basketball, bocce ball, boomerang, bowling, boxing, camping, cricket, croquet, curling, cycling (mountain biking), fencing, field hockey, fishing, foosball, football, golf, gymnastics, hackysack (foot bag), handball, hiking, hockey, horseback riding, horseshoe, hunting, inline skating, jogging, jump rope, lacrosse, martial arts (judo, ju jitsu, karate, tae kwon do), racquetball, roller-skating, rugby, running, shooting skeet and/or targets, shuffleboard, skateboarding, soccer, softball, squash, table tennis, tennis, track and field, triathlon, volleyball, walking, weight lifting, wrestling.

- Water sports - boating, jet ski, rowing, sailing, scuba, surfing, swimming and diving, water polo, water skiing, water slide, white water canoeing, windsurfing

- Winter sports - cross-country skiing, dog sled, ice fishing, ice skating, skiing, snowmobile

- Spectator sports - watching on TV or attending in person - auto racing, baseball, basketball, dog racing, football, golf, hockey, horse racing, ice-skating, rodeo, tennis (Coaching any sport)

TRAVELING AND SIGHTSEEING - amusement/theme parks, art galleries, attending plays, auctions, beaches, circus, concerts, cruises, exhibits, exploring caves, fairs, field trips for scientific study, guided tours, historical sites, mountains, museums, parks (both local and national), poetry readings, recreational vehicle traveling, safari, shows, spas, theatrical productions, wine tasting.

VOLUNTEER - AMERICORP, ASPCA, big brother/big sister, blind services, campfire, citizenship tutor, community organizations, crisis-line, deaf services, disaster relief, environmental society, fire department, foster parents, fund raising, GED tutor (one-on-one), gift shop or store to support worthy cause, Habitat for Humanity, handicapped, homeless shelters, hospitals, Humane society, nursing homes, parks, political campaign, Red Cross, retired senior volunteer program (RSVP), scouts, soup kitchens, teacher's aid, telephone work for a cause, youth groups, zoos.

WORKING WITH YOUR HANDS - basket weaving, blacksmith, bookbinding, brass, cake decorating, calligraphy, candle making, cartooning, cooking, cross-stitch, decoration making, drawing, fly tying, furniture refinishing, glass work, glass blowing, home workbench or workshop, jewelry design or making, knitting, macrame, map making, metal work, miniature or model making (airplane, cars, railroad), needle work, origami, painting, paper art, pottery, puppetry, quilting, refinishing art objects, scrapbooks, sculpture, sewing, stained glass, taxidermy, toy and doll making, upholstery, watch and clock making or repair, weaving, welding, woodworking.

WRITING - articles, books, columns, creative, diary, e-mail, letters, newsletters, nonfiction, pen pals, poems, reports.

MISCELLANEOUS -

- Acting

- Baton twirling

- Beach combing

- Courtroom observation

- Dancing for fun or performance (social, tap, ballet, country- western, ballroom, belly dance, Latin, clogging, folk, square dancing)

- Dinner out

- Family/Friend outings, picnics, parties, reunions, get togethers

- Fashion design

- Garage Sales

- Genealogy (family tree)

- Ham radio, cb radio, police scanner, short-wave radio, audio components

- Home brewing

- Home garden tours, garden club

- Home movie production

- House foreign students

- Kite flying or Kite making

- Leadership training

- Library

- Movies

- Music - listening to, making (playing instrument alone/others)

- Photography - taking pictures, developing, printing, showing pictures to others, camcorder

- Playing catch (Frisbee, baseball, football)

- Playing with children

- Prospecting (gold, gems, etc.)

- Public Speaking, debate

- Publicity, public relations

- Publishing, books, magazines, newsletters

- Reading books, magazines, newspapers, etc.

- Relaxation (meditation, yoga, etc.)

- Self beautification (Jacuzzi, massage, manicure, pedicure, sauna, facials)

- Soapbox Derby

- Science (astronomy, anthropology, biology, chemistry, cosmology)

- Shopping - clothing, books, etc.

- Singing

- Story telling
- Teaching on any subject
- Telephone, talking on the
- Television, watching
- Theater production
- Treasure hunting (metal detector at beach, deep sea)

"To fill the hour - that is happiness."
Ralph Waldo Emerson

Chapter # 33: Exercise

This section reviews over 76 benefits of exercise and then offers helpful hints when starting a new exercise regimen. **REMEMBER: See your physician before beginning any exercise program.** If this list is too long to read word for word, just peruse it quickly if you prefer; the bottom line is that exercise is good for both your physical and emotional health.

Benefits:

1.   Helps you to more effectively manage stress. Biologically, exercise seems to give the body a chance to practice dealing with stress; So instead of reacting strongly to every stressful situation (i.e., tension, headache, anxiety, etc.), the body reacts in a more moderate fashion. Just as the skin forms calluses with repeated contact as a way to protect the skin, exercise can protect the body from environmental stressors.

2.   Helps you to fall asleep easier and sleep better.

3.   Helps to alleviate depression. (Physically active people have lower rates of depression than sedentary people). Exercise can help reduce depression by helping a person to accomplish short term goals, enhance energy levels, gain step-by-step mastery of an activity, and break the cycle of inactivity.

4.   Helps to alleviate anxiety. (Physically active people have lower rates of anxiety than sedentary people). Exercise can help to relieve the physical signs of tension and anxiety.

5.   Assists you in your efforts to stop smoking.

6.   Helps you to combat substance abuse.

7.   Improves your general mood state. The primary mood effect of moderate exercise is energy enhancement; a secondary effect is tension reduction.

8.   Improves self-esteem.

9.   Gives you more energy and vigor to meet the demands of your daily life, and provides your with a reserve to meet the demands of unexpected emergencies.

10.   Helps you to relax.

11.　Helps relieve the pain of tension headaches - perhaps the most common type of headache.

12.　Helps to relieve and prevent "migraine headache attacks."

13.　Produces endorphins; the brain's natural pain killers.

14.　Helps to boost creativity.

15.　Increases your productivity at work.

16.　Improves your decision making abilities.

17.　Reduces work days missed due to illness.

18.　Helps improve short-term memory in older individuals.

19.　Improves your mental alertness.

20.　Improves mental cognition - a short-term effect only.

21. WEIGHT:

- Helps you to lose weight.
- Improves your body's ability to use fat for energy during physical activity.
- Helps you to maintain your weight loss - unlike dieting alone.
- Helps you to burn excess calories.
- Allows you to consume greater quantities of food and still maintain caloric balance.
- Protects against "creeping obesity" (the slow, but steady weight gain that occurs as you age).
- Reduces your level of abdominal obesity "spare tire" - a significant health risk factor.
- Helps decrease your appetite - a short-term effect only.

22.　BLOOD PRESSURE:

- Reduces your risk of developing hypertension (high blood pressure).
- Helps control blood pressure in hypertensives.
- Reduces the rate and severity of medical complications associated with hypertension.
- Offsets some of the negative side effects of certain antihypertensive drugs.
- Decreases (by 20-30 percent) your need for antihypertensive medication, if you are hypertensive.

23. Reduces your risk of developing colon cancer.

24. Reduces your risk of developing breast cancer.

25. Reduces your risk of developing prostate cancer.

26. Reduces your risk of having a stroke.

27. Improves the functioning of the body's immune system.

28. Improves overall physical health.

29. Helps you to incur fewer medical and health care expenses.

30. Increases your ability to supply blood flow to your skin for cooling.

31. Increases the diffusion capacity of your lungs, enhancing the exchange of oxygen from your lungs to your blood.

32. Reduces the viscosity of your blood.

33. Expands your blood plasma volume.

34. Helps to relieve constipation.

35. Improves your heat tolerance.

36. Increases your ability to adapt to cold environments.

37. Helps you to maintain your resting metabolic rate.

38. Provides you with protection from injury.

39. Improves your ability to recover from physical exertion.

40. May extend life span.

41. Improves your athletic performance.

42. Reduces your risk of gastrointestinal bleeding.

43. <u>HEART:</u>

- Reduces risk of heart attack/heart disease.

- Improves the likelihood of your survival from a myocardial infarction (heart attack).
- Improves your coronary (heart) circulation.
- Reduces your vulnerability to various cardiac dysrhythmias (abnormal heart rhythms).
- Lowers your resting heart rate.
- Increases your cardiac reserve.
- Increases your stroke volume (the amount of blood the heart pumps with each beat).
- Reduces your susceptibility to coronary thrombosis (a clot in the artery that supplies the heart with blood).
- Makes your heart a more efficient pump.

44.   Improves your body posture.

45.   Increases the density and breaking strength of your bones.

46.   Helps to retard bone loss as you age, thereby reducing your risk of developing osteoporosis.

47.   Increases the density and breaking strength of your ligaments and tendons.

48.   Increases the thickness of the cartilage in your joints.

49.   Slows the rate of joint degeneration if you suffer from osteoarthritis.

50.   Improves your pain tolerance and mood, if you suffer from osteoarthritis.

51.   Maintains or improves your level of joint flexibility.

52.   Helps prevent and relieve the stress that cause carpal tunnel syndrome.

53.   Helps the body resist infection of the upper respiratory tract.

54.   Improves balance and coordination.

55.   Helps you to overcome jet lag.

56.   Reduces your likelihood of developing low back problems.

57.   Helps to alleviate low back pain.

58. Helps you to maintain an independent lifestyle.

59. Improves your physical appearance.

60. Increases your circulating levels of HDL (good) cholesterol and reduces your circulating levels of triglycerides.

61. MUSCLE:

- Increases endurance and preserves muscle mass.
- Increases your level of muscle strength.
- Increases your anaerobic threshold allowing you to work or exercise longer at higher intensity before a significant amount of lactic acid builds up.
- Improves your respiratory muscle strength and muscle endurance - particularly important for asthmatics.
- Enhances your muscles' ability to extract oxygen from your blood.

62. Enhances sexual desire, performance and satisfaction.

63. Can protect you from injuries.

64. Eases the discomfort of arthritis.

65. Increases your maximal oxygen uptake; perhaps the best measure of your physical working capacity.

66. Helps you to preserve lean body tissue.

67. Improves your glucose tolerance.

68. Reduces your risk of developing Type II (non-insulin-dependent) diabetes.

69. Increases your tissues' responsiveness to the actions of insulin (i.e., improves tissue sensitivity for insulin), helping you to better control your blood sugar - particularly if you are a Type II diabetic.

70. Helps reduce the amount of insulin required to control your blood sugar level if you are a Type I (insulin-dependent) diabetic.

71. Helps to alleviate certain menstrual symptoms.

72. Reduces your risk of endometriosis (a common cause of infertility).

73.   Helps relieve many of the common discomforts of pregnancy (i.e., backache, heartburn, constipation, etc.).

74.   Physically active elderly people perform better than sedentary elderly people on cognitive tasks such as reasoning, vocabulary, memory and reaction time (Robert Dustman, Ph.D., Salt Lake City, VA).

75.   If the exercise is in a group format, it can promote social activity.

76.   Improves your overall quality of life.

REMEMBER: See your physician before beginning any exercise program.

Perform moderate aerobic exercise as many times per week as possible (everyday if you can) for about 30 minutes each session. Remember, household activities (vacuuming, mowing the lawn, etc. count as physical exercise).

- Do exercises which you enjoy and are easy to perform. This will increase your likelihood of sticking with them.

- Doing exercises/sports with others can be more fun than solitary exercise, and can also act as a great motivator to keep you exercising regularly.

- Exercising in water (like a pool) will have less impact on your bones and ligaments than some other exercises.

Typical exercises include:

1. Walking
2. Running
3. Swimming
4. Tennis
5. Cycling
6. Hiking
7. Cross-country skiing
8. Weight-lifting
9. Organized sports (hockey, soft-ball, etc.)

Of course, there are many other exercises other than those listed above.

Here are some tips to follow when beginning an exercise program.

1. If you haven't had a physical examination recently, it would be a good idea to get one prior to beginning any exercise regimen.

2. Start slow and pace yourself. Begin your exercise program gradually. After becoming accustomed to a certain level of exercise, increase the level slowly.

3. Listen to your body. Occasional minor stiffness in the morning after exercise is to be expected. It is a sign that you are getting into shape. Soreness may be a sign that you overdid it. You may need to cut back a little, so go slow and easy.

4. Warm up and cool down. Like an engine on a cool morning your body needs a chance to warm up. A warm-up gradually prepares your body for exercise. Warming up is especially important for exercise that requires quick bursts of effort, such as basketball or racquet sports. Take five minutes before you participate and slowly stretch the muscle groups you will be using. When you finish your workout, your body needs a chance to cool down slowly. This means you should take five minutes at the end of your routine to let your heart gradually return to its resting rate. Keep moving at a slower pace to cool down.

5. Overdoing any exercise can do more harm than good. Exercise is good for you, but if you overdo it you may unknowingly cause harm. The most common injuries are pulled muscles and strained joints and ligaments.

"Happiness belongs to the self-sufficient."

Aristotle

Chapter # 34: Pros and Cons of Drugs That are Taken to Improve Your Mood

Drugs are simply different chemicals that interact with your body. Chemicals are produced both inside your body (i.e., endogenous) and outside your body, and can subtly (or radically) alter your mental state. These chemicals can produce a variety of physiological and psychological effects, some desirable (pleasurable sensations); others not desirable (e.g., side effects, addiction).

Brain chemistry can be altered through:

1. Medications
2. Experiences we have

In general, it is preferable to alter the level of various endogenous chemicals in the brain (neurotransmitters) through our behaviors and thoughts rather than externally, using man-made drugs. Changing brain chemicals through psychological means produces little or no side effects, and often the effects are more robust.

The following sections refer specifically to *psychotropic drugs*, or drugs which are used to alter mental functioning (i.e., mood, consciousness, activity level, etc.).

1. People use psychoactive drugs to:

- Lessen anxiety.
- Alleviate depression.
- Numb emotional pain.
- Give them confidence.
- Lower inhibitions.
- Alter consciousness.
- Relax.
- Get high.
- Decrease appetite.
- Improve sleep.
- Stabilize mood.
- Escape from problems.
- Reduce psychotic symptoms (e.g., hallucinations).

2. What are the positive features of psychotropic drugs?

- They often work fast.
- No effort is required of the person taking them.

3. What are the negative features of psychotropic drugs?

- Some drugs are physiologically and psychologically addictive. That is, a tolerance is built up in the body so a person needs more of the drug to induce the same level of effect. Also, withdrawal of the drug induces physiological and psychological distress.
- All drugs have side effects, from minimal to incapacitating.
- For many drugs, long-term effects on the body are unknown and potentially dangerous.
- There are many unknown interaction effects when taking more than one medication at a time.
- Some drugs which are used over many years can cause permanent, lethal results; Cigarettes kill 420,000 prematurely each year; Alcoholism produces many physical problems (Cirrhosis, Korsakoff's syndrome, gout, etc.)

4. Legal vs. illegal drugs:

- Legal drugs come in both prescription and non-prescription forms:

  - Prescription drugs include antidepressants, anti-anxiety agents, mood stabilizers, etc. prescribed by a doctor.

  - Non-prescription drugs include over the counter medications, herbal concoctions (seen in health food stores), drugs like caffeine found in foods and drinks (soda, chocolate, coffee), alcohol, and nicotine (cigarettes).

- Illegal drugs:

  - Other than the immediate mood altering experience they induce, illegal drugs have many pitfalls.

    a. Since they are illegal, there is a risk of arrest and incarceration with all the ramifications inherent in that process.

    b. Since these drugs are not inspected for quality or purity, the risk of them being laced with potentially lethal ingredients is present.

    c. There is always the risk of addiction and/or overdose occurring with these drugs.

    d. Driving cars and using these drugs is dangerous to both the user and potential victim outside of the car.

  e. Some drugs administered intravenously with shared needles pose the risk of getting diseases like Hepatitis and AIDS.

5. The Placebo Effect

The placebo effect is the belief of a person that a certain drug, action, or behavior will produce a desired effect. In fact, most studies on the effectiveness of drugs use a placebo control (i.e., compare the effects of the drug to a sugar pill or placebo). Surprisingly, some placebo's are quite effective. It is the job of the drug-maker to prove that his drug is more effective than a placebo. In some studies of antidepressants, placebos improve symptoms by as much as 30%, while the active drug may produce improvements of only 50%. With a placebo, the belief of the person actually produces physiological changes within the brain. There is no active ingredient other than the person's belief. With many drugs it is hard to know how much of the drug's action is due to the active ingredient, and how much is due to the person's belief.

6. Should drugs be used instead of, or in conjunction with psychotherapy?

The answer to this question depends upon whom you ask. Some mental health professionals believe psychotherapy is superior to medications, others feel the opposite, and still others feel a combination of both is superior. Research on this question is still debatable at this point.

Nevertheless, psychotropic medications:

- Do work relatively fast (except for some antidepressants which may take up to 3 weeks to work).
- Are easy to take.
- Can be the treatment of choice for people unable or unwilling to get counseling.

7. Psychotropic medications <u>do not</u>:

- Help people gain insight into **why they act as they do** (See Chapter # 30).
- Teach people to be more **assertive** (See Chapter # 21).
- Help people get their **needs** (See Chapter # 03) met in a healthy way.
- Help people **get out** (See Chapter # 22) of hurtful relationships.
- Teach people coping skills.
- Teach people to deal **more effectively with others** (See Chapters # 20-21).
- Teach people how to **solve problems** (See Chapter # 40) effectively.
- Teach people to **live healthier lives** (See Chapter # 50).

- Teach people how to **manage their time** (See Chapter # 39) more effectively.
- Help people to find **meaning** (See Chapter # 46) and a sense of personal **identity** (See Chapter # 45).

Psychotherapeutic or Self-Help methods can promote the above mentioned 10 goals. Chances are if a person is depressed or anxious due to a deficiency in one of these areas, then medications will be of minimal help in the long run. The medications may be helpful on a short-term basis, but if no improvement is made in these 10 areas, symptoms may return. That is why Psychotherapy or Self-Help may have more long-lasting effects than medications. Long-term treatment with medications may be indicated when a person is unwilling or unable to engage in psychotherapy or self-help.

8. Facts about prescription psychotropic medications

- Selling drugs is very profitable for both physicians and pharmaceutical companies. For example, sales of Prozac in 1995 exceeded $2 billion.

- Medications pose a potential risk to the fetus' of pregnant women who are unaware of their condition (70% of all antidepressants are prescribed for women).

- Many drugs prescribed for children have not been tested for efficacy on children. They have only been tested on adults. Such drugs may also pose risks to developing bodies.

- Most psychotropic medications have been tested for short periods of time (e.g., 4 months). Long-term follow-up (18 months) studies on some drugs (e.g., antidepressant, anxiolitics) indicate some of these drugs are no more effective than a placebo.

- Many people who are prescribed medications often do not take them as prescribed. They stop taking them prematurely, take fewer pills than prescribed, or don't take them at regular intervals.

Chapter # 35: Pets Can Improve Your Quality of Life

People adore pets because they are:

- Loving

- Accepting

- Affectionate

- Consistent

- Provide unconditional positive regard

- Are always there for you

- Are good listeners (no back-talk)

- They also enable a person to nurture another living thing. (Of course, some pets take more time and expense than others. Remember, a pet can be a long-term commitment).

- Research indicates that interacting with a pet can lower **blood pressure** (See Chapter # 57) and invite a state of relaxation. Pets can include dogs, cats, birds, or even watching aquarium fish.

- Pets can be a good source of social support.

- A study by Judith Siegel found that people who own pets made significantly fewer trips to the doctor than those with no animals in their lives.

- For some people, pets can have a buffering effect against stress.

"Happiness is a warm puppy."
Charles Schulz

Chapter # 36: Volunteer

Volunteering has many benefits to both the provider and recipient. Doing for others increases our **self-esteem** (See Chapter # 58), and makes us less preoccupied with ourselves. It can potentially increase our amount of social contact. Also, it can provide more **meaning** (See Chapter # 46) in one's life and help shape our **identity** (See Chapter # 45).

There is evidence that personally helping someone makes people feel good--calm, less stressed, and self-satisfied; something like a "runner's high." The benefits from helping others are less likely to occur when you:

- Merely give money
- Pay taxes
- Help without having close personal contact
- Feel compelled to help (Luks, 1988).

Examples of Ways to Volunteer

- Mow the neighbor's lawn when they are on vacation or have a death in the family.
- Help a friend move.
- Offer your friendship to a new person in school or your community.
- Offer to baby-sit for a family who can't afford a sitter.
- Take an old person to the grocery store each week or to his/her doctor; give some flowers to someone, etc.

Or try one of the following organizations:

AMERICORP, ASPCA, Big Brother/big Sister, Blind Services, Campfire Girls, Citizenship Tutor, Community Organizations, Crisis-line, Deaf Services, Disaster Relief, Environmental Society, Fire Department, Foster Parents, Fund Raising, GED Tutor (One-on-one), Gift Shop or Store to Support Worthy Cause, Habitat for Humanity, Handicapped, Homeless Shelters, Hospitals, Humane Society, Nursing Homes, Parks, Political Campaign, Red Cross, Retired Senior Volunteer Program (RSVP), Scouts, Soup Kitchens, Teacher's Aid, Telephone Work for a Cause, Youth Groups, Zoos.

"A sound mind in a sound body is a short but full description of a happy state in this world."

John Locke

Chapter # 37: See Your Doctor to Rule Out a Physical Problem

The body-mind connection is very complex and is bi-directional. This means that your emotional state can affect your physical health. The reverse is also true; various physical illnesses can promote or mimic various psychological syndromes. An example would be a thyroid condition presenting as an anxiety disorder. Therefore, it is a good idea to rule out the presence of a physical illness before beginning a non medical course of treatment (i.e., psychotherapy or self-help) by seeing your physician.

"Happiness consists in activity. It is a running stream, not a stagnant pool."
Oliver Wendell Holmes

Chapter # 38: Benefits of Relaxation, Ways to Relax

There are a variety of ways to relax. Some methods may be more effective than others for you. Also, some methods require the assistance of a mental health professional (i.e., hypnosis, biofeedback). All methods, though, should cause the same basic physiological state. Relaxation is usually associated with the following physiological markers: Reduced heart rate, elevated temperature of fingers and feet, reduced blood pressure, reduced use of sweat glands, and slow, steady breathing.

Benefits of relaxation:

- Reduces effects of stress
- Helps boost **immune** system (See Chapter # 56)
- Helps reduce **anxiety** (See Chapter # 51)
- Improves physical health
- May increase **longevity** (See Chapter # 55)
- May increase creativity and productivity at home and work

How do you know if you are relaxed or not? If you answer YES to many of the following questions, you may need to spend some time each day utilizing a relaxation technique.

- Do you hesitate to take time out to do "Nothing"?
- Do you find it difficult to unwind?
- Do you feel guilty when you take time to relax?
- Do your hands or feet get cold even in a warm room?
- Are your palms or brow chronically moist?
- In the course of the average day, do you often experience tightening of the stomach muscles?
- Rapid heartbeat?
- Shortness of Breath?
- Trembling hands or fingers?
- Restless legs?
- Are your muscles--particularly arms, legs, neck and shoulders tensed excessively and/or chronically?
- Do you clench your jaw or grind your teeth frequently?
- During a lull in your day, do you have difficulty "turning off" the pressures and just "letting go"?

Here are some different ways of relaxing. Try out different techniques and see which one works the best for you.

Breathing Exercises (See Below for 4 Different Breathing Exercises)

1. Deep Breathing

- <u>Why Deep/Abdominal Breathing?</u> When we breathe in (inhale), our diaphragm (located just above our stomach) drops and our lungs drop and fill with air. A slight expansion of the chest completes the filling of the lungs. When stressed, we tend to breathe only in our upper chest - a shallow breathing. Shallow breathing gets rid of only part of the toxins that build up in our bodies from normal cellular functions. As the day progresses, the level of toxins can build until they alone become stress inducing, so more stress results. Full, diaphragmatic/abdominal breathing which helps with more complete cleansing, is calming for many. Also, the more complete oxygen exchange helps provide us with more natural energy.

- <u>How to breath deeply.</u> Correct deep breathing should be done with your belly muscles. The idea is to let your stomach go out as far as possible as you inhale. In this way you will fill your lungs more completely. Put a hand on your abdomen and, as you inhale deeply, feel your stomach expand as though it were being filled like a balloon. Now let the air out and feel your stomach return to its normal position. As you do the exercise, pause comfortably at the end of each exhalation until you feel ready to take the next deep breath.

  Stand or sit straight, put one hand on your chest and the other on your navel ("belly button"). Now, breath so that only the hand on your navel moves - as you inhale the hand moves out, then moves in as you exhale. The upper hand on your chest does not move. Watch them as you breathe and see if you can breathe with only the lower hand moving.

2. Breathing Tension Away

  Gently focus your attention on your feet. As you take in a slow, deep breath, imagine collecting all the tensions in your feet and legs, breathing them into your lungs and expelling them as you exhale. Then, with a second deep breath, imagine all the tensions in your trunk, hands and arms, and then expel them. With a third one, collect and expel all those in your shoulders, neck and head. With practice, some persons can collect tensions in the entire body in one deep inhalation, then expel them all at once. Then, if necessary, breath away any remaining areas of tension.

3. Equalizing Breathing

- <u>Why equalize your breathing?</u> As tenseness begins, our breathing often becomes irregular, our breaths in and out shorter. Slowing down and equalizing our breathing is calming.

- <u>How to equalize your breathing.</u> *Take 4 seconds to breath in and 4 seconds to breath out. That is, as you inhale, count "1 one thousand, 2 one thousand, 3 one thousand, 4 one thousand." And, as you breath out, count similarly. Do that 4 or 5 times.*

4. Cool Air in, Warm Air Out

- <u>Why air in and out?</u> Focusing on a physiological process (breathing air in and out) can help calm our mental activity, which in turn, can result in physical relaxation. As we occupy our minds with thoughts that stress us, our bodies become stressed. Breathing is a non-mental activity and focusing our thoughts on it helps us let go of stressful thoughts. Then we can come back and deal with our daily activities in a more relaxed and productive state. Also, if you are one of those people who are bothered by racing thoughts that sometimes are difficult to control, try using the following technique when you want a mental rest.

- <u>How to perform the Cool Air in, Warm Air Out Technique.</u> *With your eyes closed, shift your attention to the tip of your nose. As you breath in, become aware of the air coming in your nostrils. As you breath out, be aware of the sensations of the air passing back out. Perhaps you notice that the air coming in tends to be cooler and the air breathed out tends to be warmer. Just be aware of the cool air in; warm air out. Do this several times.*

Muscle Relaxation - The Tense and Release Method

- <u>Why tense and release your muscles?</u> Many of us tend to tense our muscles too much during the day. So releasing the tension is relaxing. The reason for first tensing the whole body is to accentuate the feelings of relaxation when releasing the tension.

- <u>How to tense and release.</u> *You will tense yourself all over, one part at a time, while slowly moving up your body. Lie down or sit in a comfortable position. Close your eyes and take a few deep breaths. Tighten your feet and toes and hold them tight for about three seconds (bend your toes up as if to touch your shins and hold them there), then relax them. Repeat this exercise (tense, hold, and release) for your calves, thighs, buttocks, stomach muscles, chest, fists and arms. Keep moving up your body, finishing with your jaw (clench your teeth), eyes, and scalp muscles. After you complete this exercise, wait a few moments. Then open your eyes. Feel the difference?*

The Heavy Feet Method

- Why imagine that your feet are heavy? Many persons report that as they become more relaxed, they feel heaviness in parts of their body. So, one way to help us relax is to imagine that heaviness for a short time.

- How to perform the Heavy Feet technique. *Just imagine that your feet and legs are getting heavier and heavier with each breath out. It's almost as if you are wearing lead boots. Say to yourself, "My feet are heavy", "My feet are heavy." Just imagine this for a few seconds. Or, perhaps imagining heaviness in some other part of our body works for you. Do this technique while seated.*

The Hand Warming Method

- Why imagine that your hands are warm? As we become more and more relaxed, the blood vessels in our hands relax and expand. That permits more blood to flow into the hands and more blood results in warmer hands. The reverse is also true - as we become tense, our hands become cooler; and blood rushes from the extremities to the center of our bodies. The exercise of visualizing warmer hands seems to be as effective for many people as any relaxation technique.

- How to perform the Hands Warming technique. *Visualize your hands as warm - relaxed and warm. You might imagine them in a bucket of warm water, near a fire, or in warm fleece-lined gloves.*

Relax with your imagination

- *Lie down or sit in a comfortable position. Close your eyes and take a few deep breaths. Take a moment to create, in your mind's eye, an ideal spot to relax. You can make it any place, mountains, beach, real or imagined. For example, imagine enjoying yourself at the beach- listening to the waves breaking on the shore, watching the seagulls circling overhead, or going for a swim. When you have relaxed, come back from your favorite place by slowly opening your eyes.*

Relax in a meditative way

1. *Find a comfortable, quiet place with few distractions.*

2. *Choose a time when you are unlikely to be bothered or disturbed by other people.*

3. *Choose a word or phrase to repeat, either silently or aloud, while*

practicing your relaxation.

4. *Develop a passive "let it happen" attitude while practicing.*

5. *Select a comfortable position. A soft chair is probably good; if you lie down you might fall asleep. (The lotus position with crossed legs isn't necessary)*

7. *Close your eyes.*

8. *Relax all your muscles as fully and as deeply as possible.*

9. *Breathe easily and naturally through your nose. Become aware of your breathing. As you breathe out say "one" or your special word, either silently or out loud. For example breathe in.. then out, "one," breathe in .... breathe out, "one," and so on.*

10. *Continue for 10-20 minutes. Open your eyes to check the time if you wish, but don't use an alarm. When you finish, sit quietly for several minutes, at first with your eyes closed and later with your eyes open. Do not stand up for a few minutes.*

Other Ways to Relax

- **Exercise** (See Chapter # 33) - While exercising, you may not feel relaxed, but afterwards you should.

- **Listen to favorite music** (See Chapter # 08) or try new music which you find relaxing.

- **Take a shower or bath** (See Chapter # 10) to feel more relaxed.

- **Perform a favorite hobby or other activity** (See Chapter # 32) which you find relaxing.

- **If you are spiritual, prayer** (See Chapter # 29) may help you to relax.

- **The best way to fight stress is by adopting a more relaxed attitude about everything:**

  ‣ **Laugh** at yourself (See Chapter # 41)

  ‣ Have realistic **expectations** of others (See Chapter # 27)

  ‣ Try to **Accept uncontrollable situations** (See Chapter # 23)

- Try to **adopt a positive outlook** on life (See Chapter # 28)

Chapter # 39: Organize Your Life, Priorities, and Time

There are only 24 hours in a day. Of those 24 hours you will inevitably spend a good hunk of time sleeping, eating, bathing, doing chores, and other mundane tasks. The other remaining hours will be filled with work, childcare, exercise, leisure activities, etc. You will have to decide what you want to do during those hours. There are two main components to consider: What are your goals and how do you implement those goals.

Establish your goals.

Benefits of establishing your goals:

- Doing more of what you really want to do, not exclusively what others want you to do

- Having direction in your life

- Ultimately being happier

Decide what you *really* want out of life and plan what you need to do to achieve those goals. Write down specifically what you want to accomplish. Remember, consider your **needs** (See Chapter # 03) and what you find **meaningful** (See Chapter # 46). Try to spend your time on what you consider important and avoid those things that are not important to you.

- Spend your time doing those things you value or those things that help you achieve your goals.

- Draw a pie chart of how you want to spend your time. Consider how much time you would like to spend on each of the main areas of your life. The chart does not have to be a description of what you should do minute-by-minute, but rather a global outline, which, of course, you can change over time.

- Are your goals realistic? Are you planning more than you can realistically accomplish or setting unrealistic goals (i.e., setting yourself up for failure?)

- Is your plan balanced? Are you leaving time for leisure, spending time with family, exercise, etc. If not, you may want to reassess your goals. Remember, you cannot do everything! Analyze where your time goes and how long each activity takes.

- When making a decision, use **problem solving** (See Chapter # 40) as a way to make a logical, thoughtful decision. For example, write down pros and cons for goals you might want to accomplish and evaluate if you really want these goals.

Implement your goals.

Benefits of Being Organized:

- Save time

- Reduce stress

- Produce more

Nuts and Bolts: Techniques to help you carry out your goals.

- **Try not to procrastinate**. The hardest part of doing something is getting started.

- **Try to get into a routine**. If everything you do is routine, then life becomes dull, but routine does have its place. You are more likely to do things if you set aside the same time everyday to do what you need to do.

- **You cannot meet everyone's expectations**. There are times when you will have to set limits on what you are willing to do (i.e., say no when asked to do something). This is harder for some people than others. If you can't say no when asked to do things, you may be overwhelmed with too much to do, and not do anything well. You need to protect your time by saying "no" to various interruptions, activities, requests, or persons. (See Chapter # 21).

- **Everything has its place**. Put things away in an organized fashion where you can find them readily. Just being neat in your house/place of work will save you time when trying to find things, and make a favorable impression on others.

- **Make lists of things to do**; don't say I'll remember to do that later. Cross things off the list as you accomplish them.

- **Use a calendar/appointment book** and write down your appointments when you make one.

- **Use a system of files** to find important papers, documents, etc.

- **Break tasks down into small steps**. They will be less overwhelming and you will get a feeling of accomplishment each time you complete a segment. Be aware of the importance of rewarding yourself for progress. All tasks can be divided into smaller segments suitable for reward as they are accomplished.

- **Perfectionism can slow you down tremendously**. There is nothing wrong with pursuing excellence, but there comes a time when not much is gained from putting in a great deal more effort.

- **Schedule a regular time to plan your activities**. Some people find it helpful to plan their day first thing in the morning. For others, it may be better to plan in terms of a week. The minutes spent in planning will be saved many times over. It is also useful to review your priorities from time to time.

- **Prioritize your activities**. Evaluate what must be done within a given time frame and determine what can be postponed.

- **Be realistic and flexible**. You may not accomplish everything you want in the time frame you have set. Consider that you may have to change plans at the last minute.

- **Take advantage of times when your energy levels are at their highest** and do your most demanding work at those times.

- **Experiment**. Try different ways of accomplishing things and see what works for you and what doesn't. For example, some people can concentrate better at tasks with music playing in the background. For others, music is too distracting.

Troubleshooting

Deciding on my goals sounds great, but I have many responsibilities and can't think of myself only.

That's true and no one says you should think of only yourself. Your goals may include spending more time with loved ones. Your goals and your families' goals may even overlap. Discuss your goals with your family (if you feel comfortable doing so) and see if there are ways you and your family can all achieve your respective goals (i.e., help each other out).

I can't say no when others ask me to do things because they won't like me.

Well, everyone will not like you even if you always say, "Yes." If you always say, "Yes," you will inevitably be stressed out, not get everything done anyway, disappoint yourself and others, and possibly hold resentment towards those individuals requesting your services. You probably need to be more **assertive** (See Chapter # 21).

I'm too busy to spend time organizing.

Well, if you are satisfied with how you spend your time and get things done to your satisfaction using your present system of organization, that's great. If you're not, you may want to skip one television show per week and try some of the suggestions given here.

These suggestions sound nice, but I spend most of my time working to feed and clothe my family. My ideal goals and my real life are very far apart. How am I supposed to achieve these goals if I have no time or money to do so?

Well you are not alone. Many people feel this way and there is no easy magical way to transform your life. It will take slow, incremental progress and much persistence. If you feel very overwhelmed, you may want to consider speaking with a therapist or coach to help you sort out your goals.

Chapter # 40: How to Solve Problems Effectively

When you are faced with a situation, problem, or opportunity to resolve, there are certain steps which may help you make a better decision. The following information should be helpful.

How do you know you have a problem?

- You are experiencing **negative feelings** (See Chapter # 06), or your **social** (See Chapters # 18-22), **financial** (See Chapter # 61), **occupational** (See Chapter # 59), **physical** (See Chapter # 07), or academic functioning is impaired.

- Many other people tell you that you have a problem (friends, relatives, co-workers).

Once you acknowledge having a problem, you can:

<u>Avoid the problem</u>

- **Benefits of avoiding the problem**

  ▸ It's initially easy.

  ▸ Although the problem may be distressing, it is a known commodity (and may even be comfortable in a way). Facing the problem is probably unknown territory and is somewhat scary.

  ▸ Some needs are being met by avoiding change. Usually problem situations are not all bad. There may even be some positive aspects to avoiding change.

- **Drawbacks of avoiding the problem**

  ▸ The problem usually doesn't go away.

  ▸ The problem may get worse.

  ▸ You may feel powerless.

  You may want to identify the costs, feelings, and consequences of not solving your particular problem.

- **Why do we avoid the problem?** There are many reasons why people avoid problems:

- ▸ The above mentioned benefits of avoiding problems.

- ▸ Fear of the unknown.

- ▸ Fear of rejection by others.

- ▸ Fear of being judged negatively by others.

- ▸ Fear of failure.

- ▸ Feeling personally incapable of making changes.

- ▸ Feeling that addressing the problem may take too much effort (time, money, emotional energy, etc.)

- ▸ Fear that the "worst" may happen (i.e., your worst fears).

Clarify the nature of the problem

- ■ Take time to think, preferably in a quiet place about what the problem is; some problems are easier to figure out than others.

- ■ Talk to an objective person about the problem.

- ■ Ask yourself if the problem is related to a place, person, time or situation.

Face the problem - now that you recognize that indeed there is a problem, state what the problem (s) is/are as clearly and concisely as possible.

Write down as many possible solutions that you can think of, regardless of how goofy they may seem. This "brainstorming" allows you to think freely without self-censorship and may encourage a novel approach to your problem.

Explore likely rewards/consequences for each alternative (both pros and cons).

Pick a solution. You may want to go through a process of elimination, slowly deleting those alternatives which don't seem appropriate to your situation.

Try the solution out. Make a list of the steps involved in carrying out the solution (i.e., each small step) to have a clear picture of what you will be doing.

Decide if the solution is working

- **If it's not working:**

  ▸ Anticipate how you will handle possible setbacks or failures

    (1) You may have to give the solution more time to work.

    (2) Try something else to supplement the solution.

    (3) Reject the solution completely, and try something else.

- **If it is working**

  ▸ Keep it

Note the following suggestions:

- **Is the problem solvable?** Don't waste your time on problems that cannot be solved.

- **Try to solve one problem at a time.** Trying to solve too many problems simultaneously can be too confusing and overwhelming. If you can, stick to one problem at a time.

- **If the problem concerns someone else, there is only so much you can do** (i.e., change your own behaviors/attitude, or how you interact with that person). You can't change other people.

- **Consider getting help** from a friend, personal coach, or therapist if you are stuck for a long time in either defining the problem or solving the problem.

"Success is getting what you want.
Happiness is wanting what you get."
Dale Carnegie

Chapter # 41: Laughter Has Many Physical and Emotional Benefits

Laughter can be a great way to improve your mood. It is powerful both psychologically and physiologically. 100 laughs are equivalent to 10 minutes spent rowing (William Fry, psychiatrist, Stanford University School of Medicine).

Laughing robustly increases blood circulation, works abdominal and diaphragm muscles, raises the heart rate, gets stale air out of the lungs, and provides a massage for facial muscles. After a bout of laughter, blood pressure drops to a lower healthier level, muscles relax, and endorphins are released.

One hour spent laughing lowers levels of stress hormones like cortisol and epinephrine while the immune system grows stronger by increasing killer T cells and antibodies (Berk, Lee of Loma Linda School of Public Health in Calif).

Laughter may enhance your ability to be creative and think clearly (Alice M. Isen, Cornell University Psychologist)

Ways to Laugh more:

- Find out what makes you laugh; then pull together resources (e.g., funny books, movies, cartoons, etc.) so you will have them when you need them.

- Try not to take yourself too seriously all the time. Look for ways to find humor in your everyday activities (especially the stressful ones).

- Hang around more with funny people.

- Read funny books, comics, etc.

- Keep a file of jokes and cartoons that make you laugh. Paste up a few where you are likely to see them.

- Watch funny TV shows, movies, etc.

"Happiness is having a large, loving, caring, close-knit family in another city."

George Burns

Chapter # 42: Express Thoughts/Feelings

People express their emotions:

- <u>Verbally</u> - This is the basis for most psychotherapy; Talking about feelings and problems. By talking to an empathetic, non-judgmental person, we vent our feelings or "get things off our chest". This also gives us the opportunity to sort out issues in our minds.

- <u>Using the written word</u> - Writing down our thoughts and feelings is a form of expression. Sometimes it is easier to clarify issues when we see them in black and white on paper. Writing down the pros and cons of a decision or keeping a "feelings journal" are common forms of written expression.

- <u>Artistic expression</u> (poetry, painting, sculpture, music) - Expressing oneself artistically also can serve the same function as talking or writing.

- <u>Movement of the body</u> - Such expression can take the form of Dance, Yoga (as a method of relaxation) or exercise (as a way to reduce stress and/or gain competence in a skill (e.g., martial arts, tennis, etc.).

"Some cause happiness wherever
they go; others whenever they go."
Oscar Wilde

Chapter # 43: Stimulation/Excitation

People tend to get bored or stressed out when they experience the same level of stimulation consistently for any length of time. When you are bombarded by stimulating events, sounds, or sights for a while, you will crave some relaxation. Conversely, if you are in a relaxing, invariable, environment for a time, you will crave some stimulation. This is also why people like vacations; to break up the monotony. Novel environments can be stimulating. People utilize many things to change their level of stimulation (drugs, music, movies, etc.) as a way to be relaxed or aroused.

People also vary in the intensity of excitement they crave. Some people's idea of stimulation is reading a good book, while others jump out of airplanes or bungee jump. It is normal to seek stimulation; the key is to find safe, functional ways to meet your excitement needs. See Chapter # 32 for a list of stimulating activities.

"Happiness is nothing more than good health and a bad memory."
Albert Schweitzer

Chapter # 44: Distraction

What is distraction?

Distraction is a technique almost everyone uses to divert their thoughts or attention in a different direction. It may "get us out of our head" and into some external activity, or thinking about different things.

Uses of Distraction

- Pain management (both emotional and physical pain)

- Obsessional thinking or worrying

Types of Distraction:

Almost any activity can act as a distraction.

- Watching T.V.

- Reading a book.

- Using **relaxation** techniques (See Chapter # 38) - The basis of almost all relaxation is distraction. We focus on something (our breathing, muscles, mantra, etc.) and therefore, are not focusing on our thoughts. This "absence" of thinking induces a relaxed state; Focused thinking (e.g., a relaxing image) also distracts us from stressful thoughts.

- Talking to other people.

- Becoming engrossed in a pleasurable **activity** (See Chapter # 32).

- **Thought Stopping** - When experiencing unwanted or intrusive thoughts, picture a large STOP sign in your mind and yell (out loud or to yourself) STOP!!

"I don't know what your destiny will be, but one thing I do know: the only ones among you who will be really happy are those who have sought and found how to serve."

Albert Schweitzer

Chapter # 45: Explore Your Identity

People struggle to know who they really are. They attempt to acquire their own beliefs and values, not necessarily those of their family, friends, culture, etc. People define their identity by talking with other non-judgmental people, trying new activities, reading, etc. Identity can also be defined by one's *role* (mother, father, husband, wife, brother, sister, son, daughter), *religion* (Christian, Jew, etc.) *nationality* (American, Mexican, etc.) *heritage* (Irish, Italian, etc.) *job* (plumber, housewife, engineer, etc.), and *family background* (e.g., I'm a 4th generation McCoy originally from Ireland, etc.). Traditions and rituals also give people identity. People use all of these criteria to define who they are.

"Happiness is the meaning and the purpose of life, the whole aim and end of human existence."

Aristotle

Chapter # 46: Find Meaningful Pursuits (What Gives Life Meaning)

The following endeavors give people meaning in their lives :

- Nurturing and enjoying **personal relationships** (See Chapters # 18-22) with others (spouses, family, friends, etc.).

- Accomplishing personal and professional goals. Also look for further information on **job satisfaction** (See Chapter # 59), ways to **motivate** yourself (See Chapter # 47), and getting better **organized** to accomplish your goals (See Chapter # 39).

- Making a contribution of your time to community, country, etc. See Chapter # 36 for a list of **volunteer activities.**

- Raising children.

- Gaining an understanding of the cosmos through a spiritual (See Chapter # 29) and/or scientific explanation.

"Many people have a wrong idea of what constitutes true happiness. It is not attained through self gratification, but through fidelity to a worthy purpose."

Helen Keller

Chapter # 47: Ways to Help Motivate Yourself to Achieve Your Goals

There are many things you can do to improve your level of happiness. Of course, the easy part is knowing what to do. The hard part is *actually doing it*. Following are some suggestions for motivating yourself to accomplish your goals:

1. Write down all the positive things you will achieve by accomplishing this goal and keep them handy. Look at them often to remind yourself of all the benefits you can have. Also, you can write down all the reasons you don't want to continue doing things as you've done them before.

2. Write down reasons you may be resistant to achieving this goal (e.g., others may treat me differently, fear of the unknown, fear of rejection, etc.). Try to counteract these negative thoughts with more positive and perhaps realistic thoughts.

3. Because a lot of these goals will increase your level of happiness, they are self-reinforcing. That is, since they will bring you pleasure, you will be more likely to continue doing them.

4. Try accomplishing your goals with others (e.g., co-workers, friends, family, support groups, etc.). For example, exercising with a friend can help you to stay motivated and keep exercising. You can encourage each other to "stick with it." Also, the social interaction will make the process of achieving your goal more enjoyable.

5. Break down your goals into more manageable pieces. It may be easier to keep motivated when a goal is smaller and easier to accomplish (See Chapter 48).

6. **Reward yourself** for positive behaviors. (See Chapter # 16)

"Happiness comes when your work and words are of benefit to yourself and others."

Buddha

Chapter # 48: Make Complex Tasks More Manageable By Breaking Them Down, One Step at a Time

- Make slow, steady progress and give yourself rewards when you accomplish a small step.

- If you can't carry out a small step, break it down even further and try that small step.

- Be persistent. Keep trying until you achieve these steps and don't worry if you stumble, experience setbacks, or make mistakes along the way. This is normal and should be expected.

- It may be helpful to write down each step in detail. With effort, you can prevail.

- Remember, make sure your goal is realistic and achievable.

"The only true happiness comes from squandering ourselves for a purpose."
William Cowper

Section F: Specific Issues

"To attain happiness in another world we need only to believe something; to secure it in this world, we must do something."

Charlotte Perkins Gilman

Chapter # 49: How to Deal With Anger

WHAT IS ANGER?

Among the many feelings that people experience, anger is probably the most complex and confusing. In order to control or regulate anger, you must first understand it. The more you know about your own anger, the easier it will be to control it. Anger is a strong emotion that occurs when you feel you are being hassled, treated unfairly, or not receiving the respect you deserve. Sometimes you may even become angry at yourself for mistakes that you have made. Anger occurs more frequently when you are under stress. When you feel pressured or things are not going smoothly, anger can arise as a reaction to stressful events and circumstances. Anger is an antagonistic response. But it is different from aggression, which is action or behavior that is intended to cause harm or injury. Anger is a feeling, an emotion. By itself, it's not necessarily bad. However, because it can lead to aggression and because it can have detrimental affects on our health, work performance, and personal relationships, anger has many undesirable aspects.

POSITIVE ASPECTS OF ANGER

- Anger can give us strength and determination as it energizes our behavior in response to challenge or threat.

- Anger tells us something may be wrong and that we may need to resolve a particular situation. It is a signal that there is a problem which requires our attention.

- Anger can be a helpful way to express tension and communicate negative feelings to others.

NEGATIVE ASPECTS OF ANGER

- Anger interferes with our ability to think clearly and can cause us to act on impulse, suspending good judgment. Also, it can cause us to do something we may regret later on.

- Anger is an unpleasant emotion.

- Anger is physically upsetting. It involves a strong physiological arousal that if prolonged or too frequent can have detrimental effects on our health (suppression of the immune system, heart disease, and higher death rates from all causes).

- Anger is an antagonistic response that can lead to actions that can cause physical harm to yourself or someone else. Anger can also lead to negative consequences, (i.e., punishment or retaliation).

WHAT CAUSES ANGER?

Anger is the result of things that happen, how you perceive and experience those things, and what you do in response to them. That is, anger is a product of external factors, internal or psychological factors, and your own behavior.

- External factors. When you are under pressure, you are faced with many challenges, interruptions, annoyances, and even criticisms. These upsetting events are linked to anger, but they don't cause anger all by themselves. Whether or not you become angry is determined by how you perceive these events and how you approach and respond to them.

- Internal factors. How you react emotionally to a situation is determined by how you perceive or view that situation and by your level of tension or arousal at the time. If you are highly activated or agitated when something unpleasant happens then you are more likely to get angry, especially if you view the situation in negative or antagonistic terms.

- Behavioral factors. How you respond behaviorally to a situation affects how others react to you, as well as what gets done about the existing problem. The course of action that you take will influence whether you get angry, how long you stay angry, and if you get angry all over again.

- Situations that can make you angry (Triggers)

  ‣ Teasing, Name calling, Insults, or Inappropriate comments.

  ‣ When you get punished for something, and another person who did the same thing did not get punished.

  ‣ When someone makes a promise to you and doesn't keep it.

  ‣ When you get punished for something you didn't do.

  ‣ When you try to do the "right thing" and go about things in a proper/legal/ethical fashion and you don't get the reward you expect.

  ‣ When someone is rude or impolite.

- ► When someone else doesn't follow the rules.

- ► When someone tries to take advantage of you (e.g., always asks you for favors and never reciprocates).

- ► When someone steals from you.

- ► When someone is selfish.

- ► When a close friend/romantic partner leaves you.

- ► When someone doesn't act the way you think they ought to act.

- ► When you don't live up to your own standards.

- ► When things don't go your way (i.e., you don't get what you want)

- ► When others don't listen to you and/or ignore you.

- ► When others interrupt you and don't let you talk.

- ► A build-up of small annoyances (traffic jams, malfunctioning machines, waiting in long lines, etc.)

WHEN IS ANGER A PROBLEM?

- ■ <u>When it is too frequent.</u> Some things would make anybody angry, but when daily situations and minor events are making you angry, you are probably experiencing this emotion more than average.

- ■ <u>When it is too intense.</u> Intense anger is almost never useful. It severely reduces your ability to think clearly and leads to impulsive acts that you later regret.

- ■ <u>When it lasts too long.</u> When you can't let go of something that has upset you, it can interfere with your work and enjoyment of life.

- ■ <u>When it leads to aggression.</u> Strong anger can lead to destructive acts. Anger makes it easier to say or do something that hurts someone when you are least likely to think through the consequences of your behavior.

IDENTIFY HOW YOU CURRENTLY DEAL WITH ANGER (i.e., do you withdraw, keep the anger bottled up inside, display angry outbursts with yelling and screaming).

CONTROLLING ANGER

Anger control, when done effectively, does not mean bottling it up or keeping a tight lid on it. Anger control or anger management involves several important things:

- ▸ Learning how not to get angry in the first place.

- ▸ Learning **acceptance** (See Chapter # 23) of unchangeable situations.

- ▸ Changing **expectations** (See Chapter # 27) of others - Change your expectations of yourself and/or others. Some people have very high expectations of themselves and become angry with themselves when they don't live up to their unrealistically high standards. One way to lessen anger turned inward is to lower these expectations. Similarly, many people have unrealistic expectations of others and when others don't act as one thinks they should, anger results. If you expect others to act as you do all the time, you certainly will become angry and frustrated with them. Lowering your expectations of others will reduce the number of anger provoking situations you experience.

- ▸ Adopting a **Positive** attitude (See Chapter # 28).

- ▸ **Exercise** (See Chapter # 33) - to diminish overall stress levels.

- ▸ **Relaxation** (See Chapter # 38) - to diminish overall stress levels.

- ▸ **Stimulus Control** (See Chapter # 13) - if you can, avoid those situations that make you angry.

Keeping anger at a moderate level of intensity and expressing it constructively

- ■ When discussing something with a person, present the facts and do not hurl personal attacks or insults. Things to avoid when expressing anger:

  - ▸ Name calling

  - ▸ Violent outbursts

  - ▸ Threats

  - ▸ Put-downs or criticism

    ▸   Screaming

■ Be more **assertive** (See Chapter # 21).

■ It was once believed that talking about what makes you angry (e.g., to a friend or therapist) would dissipate the anger. Recent research suggests that this expression does not diminish anger and in some cases may exacerbate it.

■ **Distraction** (See Chapter # 44) - Remove yourself temporarily from the situation to cool down (e.g., take a walk, distract yourself) and then address the situation later on in a calmer fashion.

■ Use effective **problem-solving** (See Chapter # 40) strategies to change problematic situations.

"Get happiness out of your work or you may never know what happiness is."

Elbert Hubbard

Chapter # 50: Weight Loss and Maintenance

2Steps2Happiness: A Different Approach to Weight Control

Most weight loss programs focus on rapid initial weight loss (i.e., a diet) for a specific time period. Unfortunately, after the diet is over, the vast majority of dieters will gain the weight back because they return to their old eating and activity habits. A lot of people believe that once they lose weight they can go back to their old eating habits and still maintain their new, lower weight: This is a false belief. Weight control should be viewed as a marathon rather than a sprint. Just as you wouldn't expect to get a college degree in 2 months, you shouldn't expect to lose weight and change habits of a lifetime in 2 months. While the 2Steps2Happiness approach to weight loss may be slower than others, the goal is to permanently change your eating and exercise habits and therefore, maintain a lower weight indefinitely (not just during the diet). That's why 2Steps2Happiness Weight-Loss has a long-term focus. Moreover, slower weight loss is safer as well.

2Steps2Happiness Weight-Loss also differs from other weight loss programs by emphasizing a simpler approach: For example, most other programs emphasize counting calories. While this is not necessarily a bad idea, most people are not going to expend the time and effort necessary to count their daily caloric intake. 2Steps2Happiness Weight-Loss does not specify the number of calories to eat daily. Rather, 2Steps2Happiness Weight-Loss recommends counting how much you eat (e.g., number of slices of bread, number of nuts, tablespoons of peanut butter, cups of rice, etc.) This information can be written down or not, as long as you can remember how much you are eating. The initial part of the 2Steps2Happiness Weight-Loss program does not require you to restrict quantity of foods (see below). In general, one can eat a lot of vegetables, fruits, whole-grain carbohydrates, and smaller portions of fats. Most weight loss programs specify a low daily calorie intake (usually from 1200 to 1500 calories) for the duration of the "diet." Then, after the diet is over, calorie intake is allowed to increase. After months of restriction, most people rebound and start eating more and more until they resume their old eating habits. 2Steps2Happiness Weight-Loss concentrates initially on changing "what you eat" rather than how much you eat (quality versus quantity).

Also, the initial part of 2Steps2Happiness Weight-Loss concentrates on finding an enjoyable, easy form of physical activity. Both a change in the quality of food and an increased activity level will begin to slowly reduce your weight. When this weight loss slows down and stops, then it is time to slowly reduce the quantity or amount of food you eat. You'll have 3 figs instead of 4 or 2 slices of bread instead of 3 slices. As you reduce the quantity of food you eat, it is important to finish off the meal with a small serving of nuts (that is if you can eat nuts and are not allergic to them). You could also have a portion of avocado, some olive oil on bread, or even a small piece of chicken. The point of this is that fat satisfies your appetite and will lengthen the amount of time until you get hungry again. Gradually, over time, your body will get used to ingesting smaller quantities of food. You will lower the amount of food until you have achieved your ideal, healthy weight. Of course, you need to eat enough food to get the minimum amount of protein, fat, carbohydrates, fiber, vitamins, and minerals necessary for good health. If you decide that you would like to eat a larger quantity of food and maintain your weight, you can either eat more vegetables or increase the amount of physical activity you engage in.

Why Are So Many People Overweight?

- **Energy Equation -** The key to weight control is keeping energy intake (food) and energy output (physical activity) in balance. When you consume only as many calories as your body needs, your weight will usually remain constant. If you take in more calories than your body needs, you will put on excess fat. If you expend more energy than you take in, you will burn excess fat. You gain weight when your calorie intake (food and drink) exceeds what you expend through exercise and basal metabolism. Therefore, to lose weight, you must use up more calories than you take in.

- **Lack of Physical Activity -** People are living more sedentary lives in recent decades (cars, elevators, sitting at a desk all day, sitting on the couch, watching too much television). More than 60% of American adults do not get enough physical activity to provide health benefits. More than 25% are not active at all in their leisure time. Activity decreases with age and is less common among women than men and among those with lower income and less education. Insufficient physical activity is not limited to adults. More than a third of young people in grades 9-12 do not regularly engage in vigorous physical activity. Daily participation in high school physical education classes dropped from 42% in 1991 to 29% in 1999.

- **Eating Habits**

  - Learned Habits - Many people learn poor eating habits from their parents.

  - Eating too much - Many people eat too much food.

  - Eating High Fat Foods - Many people eat too much food high in saturated fats.

- **Medical Problems** - Only 3% of obesity is caused by medical problems, such as a thyroid problem.

- **Psychological Causes** - Some people use food as a way to reduce boredom, comfort themselves, numb their emotional pain, cope with stressors, deal with unmet human needs, etc. He or she may use food to deal with the following feelings: Depression, anger, boredom, emptiness, loneliness, feeling devalued, helplessness, inadequacy, stressed, frightened etc.

- **Genetic Causes** - Some people have a genetic predisposition to store more fat than others (metabolism) or may have an above average appetite.

- **Marketing of Fast Food** - Cheap and tasty fast food is advertised everywhere.

- **Availability of Food** - Unlike many developing countries, the United States has grocery stores and restaurants brimming with food.

Benefits of Weight Loss

- **Better Health** - Losing weight will improve your health by reducing your likelihood of getting a number of diseases.

- **Lower Health Care Costs** - It will reduce the use of medical services and prescription medications.

- **Gain Energy and Agility**- It will probably be easier for you to accomplish more daily tasks without added effort.

- **Increased Self Worth** - You will feel better about yourself (more confidence, less self-conscious).

- **Look Better** - A more youthful and attractive appearance will be yours.

- **Positive Feedback From Others** - Unfortunately, others often treat us based upon our outward appearance and a slimmer appearance will engender more positive behaviors from others.

- **Live Longer** - Numerous animal studies indicate a lower body mass increases life span and reduces age related illnesses.

Potential Negative Consequences Of Being Overweight

- Increased likelihood of being dissatisfied with your body image.

- Increased likelihood of experiencing back pain.

- Increased likelihood of experiencing shortness of breath when walking up an incline or stairs.

- Increased likelihood of being self-conscious about your body

- Increased likelihood of experiencing embarrassment when eating in a restaurant, swimming in a public place, shopping for food, or shopping for clothing.

Being overweight increases the risk of the following health problems:

- Hypertension (High Blood Pressure associated with risk of strokes)

- Abnormal blood cholesterol levels (High HDL Cholesterol) associated with risk of heart disease

- Type 2 Diabetes

- Cardiovascular Disease (coronary artery disease, peripheral vascular disease and heart failure)

- Stroke

- Gallbladder Disease

- Osteoarthritis (wearing away of the tissue that protects the joints like those of the hip, knees and back)

- Sleep Apnea (upper respiratory airways collapse during sleep resulting in loud snoring, disrupted sleep and daytime tiredness)

- Respiratory Problems

- Gout

- Urinary Incontinence

- Reproductive dysfunction

- Gastroesophageal Reflux Disease

- Endometrial, Breast, Prostate, and Colon Cancers

- Premature Death

Getting and Staying Motivated

Motivation is a very important factor in losing and maintaining body weight. A major goal of 2Steps2Happiness Weight-Loss is to move you from external motivation to internal motivation (i.e., self-motivation). This transition of motivation (i.e., external to internal) varies from person to person, and can take time. Below are some suggestions to keep you motivated:

- **Establish achievable, realistic weight loss goals to begin with.** (Don't set goals of too much weight loss or too rapid a weight loss). A loss of as little as 10% body weight can have many positive health effects.

- **Acquire and Maintain Emotional and Moral Support From Others** (Talking to other people face-to-face, by telephone or online). This can take the form of a weight loss group, a friend, a spouse, a psychologist, a coach or someone who supports your weight loss goals.

- Sometimes **competing** with a family member, a friend, or a support group will motivate you to keep on track.

- **Think of yourself as a person who lives healthily**; One who takes care of their bodies (i.e., through diet, exercise, avoiding smoking and binge drinking, etc.). If you embrace this way of looking at yourself; you are more likely to engage in healthy behaviors.

- **Maintain a Positive Attitude about accomplishing your goals** (Think of this experience as an exciting adventure; there is nothing like setting a goal and achieving it). Look at the switch to leaner foods as a chance to find new, tasty things to eat rather than as a punishing deprivation. Buy some low-calorie cookbooks, swap recipes with friends, experiment with herbs and spices, sample exotic fruits and grains, and keep searching for packaged foods that are lean and tasty.

- **Review (Daily!) the Benefits of Weight Loss**

- **Review (Daily!) the Potential Negative Consequences Of Being Overweight** (Unfortunately, sometimes it takes a serious health problem like a heart attack or warning from a physician that motivates one to change their diet and exercise behaviors).

- **Self-Rewards for Completed Goals.** Write a list of how you will reward yourself when you achieve your weight loss goals. (e.g., buy new clothing). (See Appendix # 4 to write list).

Substitution and Weight Loss

It is a good idea to find other enjoyable behaviors to substitute for "recreational eating." (See Appendix # 4) Also, you will want to substitute one food for another (See Appendix # 8).

List of Activities to Substitute For Eating (Add your own ideas on Appendix # 4)

- Listen To Music

- Exercise

- Talk to Someone

- Perform a Hobby

- Chew Gum

- Relaxation Exercises

- Other Pleasurable Activities (bath, play with your pet, etc.)

Food Substitution: Substitute One Food For Another (See Appendix # 8)

Exercise

Before beginning any exercise program, consult with your physician for possible precautions!

Introduction

Physical activity is crucial for long term weight regulation. Studies show that most people who lose weight and keep it off do some type of exercise. Also, research indicates that people are more likely to stick to an exercise routine if it is home based. This makes sense since having to go to a gym takes time, money, and effort. Many people walk in their neighborhood for exercise. Of course, walking is not always a good idea depending upon the weather, safety concerns, etc. You may want to consider the benefits of using a home-based treadmill or stationary bicycle (see below).

Advantages of Home-Based Exercises

- Convenient (Don't have to drive anywhere)
- Easy to use

- Can use regardless of weather, daylight
- Safer to use than exercising outside at night
- Don't have to rely on others (as with group sports)
- Can use while watching television or reading to make the time pass more quickly (e.g., an engrossing story like a soap opera)
- No monthly fees (as with a gym)
- Can be affordable (some stationary bicycles can be purchased for as little as $100 or used equipment could be purchased)

A Note about Weight Loss and Metabolism

Metabolism is the chemical processes in a living organism by which food is used for tissue growth or energy production. As you lose weight, your metabolism slows down (both fat and lean muscle mass are lost). Also, as you age, your metabolism slows down due to a decrease of lean muscle tissue. A slower metabolism means that your body burns fewer calories than a metabolism that is faster. One way to raise your metabolism and counteract the forces mentioned above (i.e., to maintain a lower weight) is to increase your muscle mass through resistance training. Muscles need fuel and the more muscle you have, the higher your metabolism will be; and therefore, you can eat more food without gaining weight. It is recommended that before beginning resistance training, you check with your doctor first, and after getting their O.K., consult a professional trainer (either at a health club or privately) to learn the proper technique of resistance training.

Types of Exercise

Find an activity that you enjoy, is convenient, and affordable. This will increase your likelihood of sticking with it.

- Walking is particularly attractive because of its ease and accessibility (Some people use a pedometer which tells them how many steps they take in a day; with this device they find out how far they move on an average day and then try to increase the number of steps; pedometers are relatively inexpensive - $5 plus).

- Also, try to increase "every day" activities such as taking the stairs instead of the elevator.

- Competitive sports, such as tennis, swimming, golf (if you pull a cart or carry clubs) and volleyball, can provide an enjoyable form of exercise for many. Doing exercises/sports with others can be more fun than solitary exercise, and can also act as a great motivator to keep you exercising regularly.

- Household activities (vacuuming, mowing the lawn, yard work, ironing, cooking, house cleaning) count as physical exercise! Or you could even try getting up to change the television channel instead of using the remote control. Consider eating in the dining room rather than the kitchen; you can actually burn more calories if you have to walk further to the table.

- Another alternative is to put on your favorite music and dance for exercise.

- Become a fidgeter. Several studies have shown that people who move around a lot—ambling about, tapping their feet, gesturing, swinging a leg while sitting—burn more calories and tend to be leaner overall than those who stay motionless.

Some typical exercises include:

- Walking
- Running
- Swimming
- Tennis
- Cycling
- Hiking
- Cross-country skiing
- Weight-lifting
- Organized sports (hockey, soft-ball, etc.)

Amount of Exercise

Aim for about 30 minutes or more of moderate-intensity physical activity on most, and preferably all, days of the week; although, anything is better than nothing! Thirty minutes of exercise can be one continuous session of 30 minutes or 3 bouts of 10 minutes throughout the day. Do whatever works for you. (Note: Stop exercising right away if you: have pain or pressure in the left-chest or mid-chest area or left neck, shoulder, or arm; feel dizzy or sick; break out in a cold sweat. You could hurt yourself if you ignore the pain.) If you experience any of these symptoms, call 911 immediately.

How Much Fat Does Exercise Burn?

How much exercise is needed to make a difference in your weight depends on the amount and type of activity, and on how much you eat. Aerobic exercise burns body fat. A medium-sized adult would have to walk more than 30 miles to burn up 3,500 calories, the equivalent of one pound of fat. Although that may seem like a lot, you don't have to walk the 30 miles all at once. Walking a mile a day for 30 days will achieve the same result, providing you don't increase your food intake to negate the effects of walking. If you consume 100 calories a day more than your body needs, you will gain approximately 10 pounds in a year. You could take that weight off, or keep it off, by doing 30 minutes of moderate exercise daily.

Grocery Shopping

- If you buy food and keep it at home, there is a very good chance that you will eat it.
  So, If you don't want to eat it, don't buy it!

- Read the labels as you shop and pay attention to serving size and servings per container (See Appendices # 9 and # 10).

- Use a Grocery Shopping List (See Appendix # 5).

Tracking Your Weight Loss Progress

- **Measure Your Waistline Periodically** (Health risks increase as waist measurement increases, particularly if the waistline is greater than 35 inches for women or 40 inches for men)

- **Weigh Yourself Periodically** (This will help keep you on course and provide you with important feedback to adjust your diet accordingly). For example, weigh yourself once per week in the morning. Avoid weighing yourself daily because weight fluctuates too much on a daily basis due to water retention, menstruation, hormones, etc. (See Appendix # 6)

- **Write Down What You Eat on a Calendar** (This will help you keep track of what you have eaten over the past week and help you to eat a variety of foods). (See Appendix # 6)

Characteristics of Individuals Who Have Lost Weight and Kept It Off

The **National Weight Control Registry** (NWCR) is a database of people who have self-reported a weight loss of 30 pounds or more and kept it off for at least a year. Despite extensive histories of being overweight and failed dieting attempts, registry members have lost an average of 66 pounds and maintained the required minimum weight loss of 30 pounds for an average of 5 years. Nearly every participant used diet and exercise to initially lose weight, and nearly every subject is currently using diet and exercise to maintain his/her weight loss. Registry members report that weight loss has led to significant improvements in self-confidence, mood and physical health.

- 89 percent changed their diets and increased physical activity (10 percent used diet modification only and one percent used activity only).

- 55 percent used a formal program (like a Weight Loss Support Group) or professional assistance (dietitian, psychologist, etc.).

- 87.6 percent limited some type or class of food (especially high-fat and high-calorie foods).

- 44.2 percent limited the quantities of food they ate.

- 43.7 percent counted calories.

- 92 percent exercised at home, 40.3 percent exercised regularly with a friend, and 31.3 percent exercised regularly with a group.

- Walking was the most common activity reported.

- 77 percent said a medical or emotional event triggered weight loss.

- 42.7 percent described losing weight as hard, 31.4 percent as moderately hard, and 25.7 percent as easy.

- Two-thirds were overweight as children (about 46 percent indicated that they became overweight at age 11 years or younger and 25.3 percent at 12 to 18 years).

- 46 percent had one biological parent who was overweight, and 26.8 percent indicated that both biological parents were overweight.

- 91 percent had tried to lose weight before.

Rate of Weight Loss

Loss of ½ to 2 pounds per week is usually safe. Those who are very overweight may lose more per week. It is probably best to consult with your physician to determine the safest amount of weight for you to lose per week. A weight loss of more than 2 lbs per week is not recommended because it increases the risk of excessive loss of lean body mass, nutrient deficiencies, fatigue and in some cases gallstones.

Portion Sizes

- When first changing your diet, **it may be easier to change what you eat** (Quality); Then gradually reduce the amount (Quantity) of what you eat, if necessary.

- **Eating off smaller plates** makes it look like you are eating larger portions of food.

- **Some important questions to ask yourself**: Do you eat large portions (compared to others)? Would you still be hungry if you ate a smaller portion? Do you often eat second helpings? Would you still be hungry if you ate only one helping? Do you always clean your plate (i.e., eat everything on your plate)? What would happen if you didn't clean your plate? How would you feel about eating small portions of a variety of foods (e.g., 1 fig, 1 piece of chocolate, 5 nuts, etc.) instead of a larger portion of just one food?

- Vegetables (**Eat all the leafy green vegetables you want**)!

- **Try to avoid putting more on your plate than you plan to eat.**

- There are probably some foods that are so tasty, that you cannot control yourself; You overeat them almost any time this food is available. These foods are usually sweets or salty snacks. If you are aware of such foods, do everything you can to avoid them; eat something else that is tasty and that you can control better.

- **Check product labels** to learn how much food is considered to be a serving, and how many calories, grams of fat, and so forth are in the food. (See Appendices # 9 and # 10). Sometimes, labeled serving sizes are ridiculously small to make foods look like they have less salt or fat. You may have to either eat "several servings" or in some cases less than one serving. For example, you probably would want to eat more than one serving of mixed frozen vegetables and less than one serving of nuts or chocolates.

Dealing With Hunger

- **First, ask yourself if you are genuinely hungry** or just bored, anxious, etc. If you are not genuinely hungry, consider waiting 15 minutes and distracting yourself with another activity.

- Even if you are genuinely hungry, you can **try distracting yourself** with another activity as hunger tends to wane over time.

- **Exercising** can temporarily reduce your appetite.

- **Lessening Frequency and Intensity of Hunger**- Eating foods high in sugar (e.g., cookies, cakes, sodas) or refined carbohydrates (like white bread or white rice) may cause you to get hungry more quickly because of their affect on blood sugar. Therefore, reducing high sugar foods like sodas will be helpful. Try to drink non-sugared beverages instead. Also eating whole-grain carbohydrates (e.g., brown rice or whole wheat bread), high fiber foods (e.g., beans, fruits and vegetables), and foods which have a high water content (e.g., soup, yogurt, cooked whole grains like oatmeal, rice, most fruits and vegetables) tends to keep blood sugar in a more moderate range.

- **When you do get hungry, (and it's not meal time yet) try eating a small amount of a healthy fat** like Almonds, Walnuts, Non-hydrogenated Peanut Butter, Avocado or Olive Oil to satiate your appetite. Nothing satisfies like fat, but try to make it a healthy fat like the ones mentioned above (They are low in saturated fat and have no transfat).

- Or you could even **try low-fat protein** like chicken breast, or snacks like popcorn, puffed wheat or rice, Cheerios, celery, or fruit.

- **Eat more frequently**. Consuming small, frequent meals helps keep hunger at bay (up to 5 meals per day). Some evidence suggests that light, frequent meals may even boost people's energy level and improve their mood; that may help them stick with their diet.

- **Get more sleep**. Why do people who sleep less weight more? Two hormones seem to be involved: Leptin, which is released by fat cells, signals the brain to stop eating. Ghrelin, which is made in the stomach, is a signal to keep eating. The two influence whether you go for a second helping or push yourself away from the table.
  Studies have shown that people who sleep less:

  1. **Have lower leptin levels** - lower levels means that the brain is not getting signals to stop eating and the brain interprets a drop in leptin as a sign of starvation; The brain responds by boosting hunger and burning fewer calories. That means you put on more weight even if you don't eat more food.

  2. **Have higher ghrelin levels** - higher levels means that the brain is getting signals to keep eating.

The combination of low leptin and high ghrelin is likely to increase appetite. Researchers at Columbia University in New York City found that people who slept six hours a night were 23 percent more likely to be obese than people who slept between seven and nine hours. Those who slept five hours were 50 percent more likely - while those who slept four hours or less were 73 percent more likely to be obese. The connection between hours slept and weight wasn't significant for people 60 and older, probably because the sleep problems that are so common in older people obscure the link.

Moreover, people who sleep less may also have more time to overeat.

What Are the Best Times To Eat?

Look at the timing of your meals and when you get hungry - Each person is different, but probably eating 3-5 meals per day is ideal. Changing your eating schedule, or setting up a schedule can be helpful, especially if you tend to skip or delay meals and end up overeating later on. Eating more frequent, smaller meals may keep you from eating too much at one sitting. A pattern of regular eating helps to reduce the risk of overeating.

Eating Out of the Home

In recent years, Americans consume 32% of their calories away from home - compared with 18% in the 1970s.

- If possible, **reduce your frequency of eating out at restaurants**. Restaurants tend to serve large portions. People almost always eat more when more food is on the plate. Also, most restaurants provide no nutritional information about their dishes. They tend to season and prepare foods to be tasty, not necessarily healthy or low fat.

- **Try to participate in the choice of the restaurant** and choose one that offers healthy options. If possible, ask for dressings or sauces to be served on the side. For example, you could order a salad with dressing on the side or a bowl of soup, and then split a dessert with someone else. If possible, avoid buffets or if you do go, just visit the buffet table once.

- **Consider creating a list of a few "Safe" dishes** for your favorite type of restaurants. Then don't look at the menu, and order first so you're not tempted by what others do.

- If you do go to a restaurant, **try to pick healthy options** (e.g., soup and salad) and reasonable portion sizes. You may want to ask for a half order, split a dish with a companion, or opt for a "doggy" bag.

- **Eating at a Friend's house** - When eating out at someone else's house, offer to serve the food so you can control your portion size or ask for a small portion. Fill your plate with salad or vegetables, and take only small amounts of high calorie dishes. This helps to control calories and avoids drawing attention to your weight control efforts.

Food Preparation

- **Bake, Broil, Roast, Steam, Poach** or occasionally Grill foods instead of Frying them. If you do fry, use Olive or Canola Oil.

- **Use Spices** to season food instead of butter or salt. Or use cinnamon, nutmeg and other sweet spices to flavor foods.

- **Limit salty foods** as much as possible (less than 2400 mg/day or one teaspoon). Your preference for salt may decrease if you gradually add smaller amounts of salt or salty seasonings to your food over a period of time.

- **Use butter substitutes** like "Smart Balance" which are low in saturated fats and transfats.

- When you bake, replace all or part of the butter or oil with **applesauce or prune puree**.

- **Reduce sugar in recipes** by a third or half. You can substitute prune puree, mashed bananas or unsweetened applesauce for some or all of the sugar in a recipe.

- **Use cooking spray** for frying and in place of oil or butter when you grease baking pans.

- **Use Heart Healthy oils** like Canola or Olive oil instead of Cotton-seed or Palm oil.

- **Consider chewing gum** while cooking if you tend to pick at food during preparation.

Eating Style

- **Try to eat slowly and savor your food** rather than unconsciously gulping it down. Quickly eaten food tends not to be noticed and less satisfying. One way to do this is by putting your cutlery down between mouthfuls.

- **Try to focus on what you are eating as a primary activity**. Performing other activities such as reading or watching T.V. may lead to over consumption because your attention is focused elsewhere, not on eating.

- It may be easier to control your eating by **sitting down in a set place** rather than eating in a variety of places.

Eating Triggers

What people, situations, or things make you want to eat?

- **Social situations** - like family gatherings, meetings with friends, etc. often include an "eating component." Happy celebrations, or somber ceremonies usually include food. Try to avoid "eating without thinking." If possible, focus on pleasurable social interactions rather than "recreational eating." Also, try to make healthy choices (i.e., vegetables instead of cookies). Some people feel social pressure to eat and, of course, the abundance of food is very tempting. You may feel that people will be offended if you eat moderately or you may feel like an oddball because you are the only one not overeating and overdrinking. Remember, you don't have to eat to please others and most people will not even notice what or how much you eat.

- **Family Influences** - Family members or partners may react in different ways to your new diet and exercise lifestyle. Some family members are very supportive and will even try to change their own diet and activity behaviors. Others may be jealous and even try to sabotage your weight loss efforts. If you feel that family members or your partner are consciously or unconsciously trying to hinder your weight control efforts, discuss this with your support group / treatment provider regarding possible solutions.

- **Watching Television** - Sometimes people (myself included) get the "munchies" when watching television at night. If you ask yourself, "Am I really hungry," you would probably say no. Try distracting yourself with another activity instead of eating **(Refer to previous section on Substitution and Weight Loss)**.

- **Food in plain sight** - Leaving food on the kitchen counter in plain sight is usually not a good idea. Out of sight, out of mind is a good motto. Also, try to put as many impediments between you and snacks as possible. Buy individually wrapped items instead of bulk, unwrapped items. Just unwrapping may act as a small deterrent by adding a step. Freeze snacks if possible. Leave the kitchen as soon as possible after you finish eating. The more steps between you and eating, the less likely you will snack unnecessarily.

- **Going on vacation** - You will have to decide if you want to maintain your usual eating habits or if you are willing eat freely and gain some weight for the period of the vacation. Do you think you can have an enjoyable time without eating or drinking excessively?

- **Entertaining at your home** - After preparing food for guests, send leftovers home with guests or freeze the leftovers.

- **Emotional Reasons** - Some people use food as a way to comfort themselves, numb their emotional pain, cope with stressors, deal with unmet human needs, etc. He or she may use food to cope with the following negative feelings: Boredom, depression, anger, emptiness, loneliness, feeling devalued, helplessness, inadequacy, stress, fear etc. **See Appendix # 2** to help you assess what positive coping techniques you are using now (or would like to use more in the future) to deal with stressors or unmet needs. Hopefully, you can replace emotional eating with one or more of these positive coping techniques.

- **Compulsive Eating** - Sometimes people are not particularly hungry, but they eat a lot of food very rapidly in a short period of time. Ideally, it is best to avoid this type of eating altogether by distracting yourself with other things. If you do find yourself eating compulsively, try to minimize the number of calories you ingest by eating puffed rice, wheat, etc. Even try eating one kernel at a time if possible. You could even munch on vegetables (which are nutritious and have very few calories). Chewing gum is also a good alternative.

- **Receiving Gifts of food** - if possible request healthy food. Consider giving these gifts to others.

Preparing for Potentially Problematic Situations

Try to anticipate which potentially difficult situations may arise that will impede your diet and exercise regime. For example, what will you do if others in your presence are eating "junk food." What excuses may you use to avoid exercise? What will you do if other household members are not eating a healthy diet like you and tempting food is close at hand?

Make a list of those situations in the past that have hampered your weight loss and maintenance (See Appendix # 4). Also list other situations that may arise in the future. Try to develop solutions to these dilemmas.

Here are a few potential situations. How would you deal with the following scenarios:

- A two-week vacation

- Breaking a leg and being immobilized for several weeks

- Getting an Illness

- Giving Birth and weighing more than before the pregnancy

- Giving up smoking

- Retiring from work

- Becoming unemployed

- Looking after young children at home

- Going through menopause

Foods and Drinks to Avoid (Or Consume in Moderation)

It is probably best to avoid the following foods (enjoying them once in a while as a treat is O.K.)

- **Fried foods** (e.g., potato chips, donuts, french fries)

- **Full Fat dairy products** (e.g., sour cream, cream cheese, butter)

- **Fatty meats** like pastrami, corned beef, or bacon

- **Sugared Sodas or Fruit Juices with a lot of sugar** like grape juice (even natural sugar has a lot of calories)

- **Limit Alcoholic Beverages -**

  1. **Alcohol can add a significant number of calories if drinking is frequent** (one alcoholic drink per day could add almost 10 pounds over the course of a year). Moderation is defined as no more than one drink per day for women and no more than two drinks per day for men. One drink can be: 12 ounces of regular beer (150 calories), 5 ounces of wine (100 calories), 1.5 ounces of 80 proof distilled spirits (100 calories).

  2. Also, **alcohol may lower your inhibitions** and diminish your ability to exert dietary restraint (i.e., being under the influence may impair your judgement and you may eat more than you would if sober).

  3. Finally, **alcohol can actually stimulate appetite**.

- A note about avoiding some food types altogether versus eating a moderate amount of these foods. If you are able to buy, for example, a bag of cookies and to eat 1-2 cookies per day, then you can probably control your cookie-eating behaviors. Conversely, if you buy a bag of cookies, and end up eating 7 per day or half a bag at a time, you probably should avoid cookies altogether. Perhaps there is another sweet that you can buy and control better than cookies. If, on the other hand, you would like to learn how to eat 1 cookie per day (i.e., moderation) you must develop better self control. This would be a matter to discuss with a support group or treatment provider.

Attitudes and Choices Relevant to Weight Regulation

How you think (i.e., your expectations, attitudes, beliefs and choices) about weight management can directly affect your subsequent eating and activity behaviors.

Attitudes

Try to keep a positive attitude about losing weight and keeping it off. But, as you know, it is not unusual for people to put weight back on. If you do gain some weight back, don't give up and go back to your old habits; instead think positively and redouble your efforts to take off those few pounds. Try to forgive yourself and move on. It is probably wise to stay within about 5 pounds of your healthy/ideal body weight.

Choices

Every moment of everyday you are making choices about what to do next. A lot of our behaviors seem routine or automatic, but individuals can alter their choices at any time. Consider some of the choices below regarding weight management. It may be helpful to consider the potential short and long term consequences of these choices before making a decision.

- Choices of eating versus engaging in another activity

- Choices regarding exercising or not exercising

- And if you do decide to exercise, you much choose the type of exercise, frequency, and duration

- Choices of what to put on your grocery shopping list as well as what you will actually buy at the grocery store (e.g., sausage or veggie burger)

- Choices of whether to regularly track your weight or not

- Choices regarding portion size

- Choices regarding when you will eat

- Choices regarding if you eat out at a restaurant, where you will eat out, and what your menu selection will be

- Choices of how to prepare your food (seasonings, cooking methods, etc.)

- Choices regarding where you eat in your home, how you eat, and what you do while you eat

- Choices of where to store your food (i.e., in plain sight or hidden)

- Choices regarding how you will respond to potentially problematic situations

- Choices of how much alcohol to drink

Recreational Eating

Most people do not eat just because they are hungry or because they want proper nutrition for good health. Eating as a way to be entertained and gain pleasure is very common. There is nothing wrong with this type of eating unless it is too frequent (i.e., eating too much or a lot of unhealthy foods). 2Steps2Happiness Weight-Loss does not "forbid" this type of eating completely. In fact, "recreational eating" can be most enjoyable on special occasions like birthdays, anniversaries, etc. In fact, you will savor those rich desserts or tasty morsels even more if you only eat them once in a while on special occasions. If you "eat for entertainment" regularly, though, it is time to find another enjoyable hobby to engage in.

Relapses

There will be times when you eat too much, eat a lot of sweets or snack foods, or gain some weight. This happens to everyone. Your thinking after these occurrences is very important. If you become self-critical, negative, and feel that you will never be able to control your eating, you probably will give up and return to your old eating and exercise patterns. Instead of getting down on yourself after these relapses, just tell yourself, O.K., I ate more than I should this time, but that does not mean that I have to return to my old eating habits. It is just one step backward, not a total failure. Think positively, forgive yourself, and move on.

Sample Meals

You are more likely to control your eating habits if you plan your meals and have quick and easy healthy foods that are readily available. This reduces the risk of eating between meals.

You will probably eat about 14 lunches and dinners over a one week period. Here are some suggestions:

- 3 Fish Meals (or 3 Turkey Meals)

- 2 Veggie Burger Meals (or Bean Burrito Meals)

- 1 Lean Beef Meal

- 1 Egg Meal (2 Eggs)

- 2 Soup Meals

- 3 Yogurt or Cottage Cheese Meals

- 2 Chicken Meals

- **Vegetable Side Dishes** can include: Fresh, Canned or Frozen Vegetables

- **Carbohydrate Side Dishes** can include: Beans, Green Peas, Corn, Rice, Chickpeas, Potatoes, or Pasta

Nutritious, Easy to Prepare Dinners

These are only a few suggestions for nutritious meals. You may want to get other meal ideas by looking through a health-minded cookbook.

- Mix Chicken Breast (Baked, Canned etc.), Brown Rice, and Mixed Vegetables (Fresh or Frozen) with your favorite seasoning. Finish off the meal with a serving of Nuts (e.g., almonds, walnuts, peanuts). Dessert of Fresh or Dried Fruit and a few pieces of dark chocolate.

- Place sliced hard boiled eggs on a mixed salad (green leafy lettuce, carrots, tomatoes, celery, etc.) with an olive oil and vinegar dressing. Serve with baked potatoes. Finish off the meal with a serving of Nuts (e.g., almonds, walnuts, peanuts). Dessert of Fresh or Dried Fruit and a few pieces of dark chocolate.

- Cooked pasta (spaghetti, macaroni, etc.) mixed with a Tomato based sauce (e.g., Ragu), mixed vegetables, and Ricotta Cheese. Top with Parmesan Cheese. Finish off the meal with a serving of Nuts (e.g., almonds, walnuts, peanuts). Dessert of Fresh or Dried Fruit and a few pieces of dark chocolate.

- Place your favorite canned beans (e.g., baked, kidney, northern, etc.) and reduced fat cheese in a tortilla (e.g., whole wheat, vegetable, etc.). Microwave for a few minutes and serve with a tossed green salad. Finish off the meal with a serving of Nuts (e.g., almonds, walnuts, peanuts). Dessert of Fresh or Dried Fruit and a few pieces of dark chocolate.

- Place canned salmon, tuna, or sardines on a mixed salad (green leafy lettuce, carrots, tomatoes, celery, etc.) with an olive oil and vinegar dressing. Serve with corn (on the cob, frozen, or canned). Finish off the meal with a serving of Nuts (e.g., almonds, walnuts, peanuts). Dessert of Fresh or Dried Fruit and a few pieces of dark chocolate.

- Mix Chicken Breast, your favorite beans, and Mixed Vegetables (Fresh or Frozen) with your favorite seasoning. Finish off the meal with a serving of Nuts (e.g., almonds, walnuts, peanuts). Dessert of Fresh or Dried Fruit and a few pieces of dark chocolate.

Nutritious, Easy to Prepare Lunches

- Mix your favorite fruit (e.g., bananas, peaches, strawberries, blueberries) with fat free Yogurt. Serve with whole wheat bread and non-hydrogenated peanut butter. Then have a small serving of your favorite nuts to finish.

- Enjoy a serving of soup (e.g., vegetable, chicken, lentil, etc.) with crackers or toast or Matzo; plus a slice of low-fat cheese. Top off the meal with a favorite fruit cup and a small serving of nuts.

- Enjoy a tossed green salad (e.g., lettuce, tomato, celery, carrots, olives, green pepper, etc.) with crackers or toast or Matzo; plus a slice of low-fat cheese. Top off the meal with a favorite fruit cup and a serving of nuts.

- Make your own Pizza. Take a slice of bread, spread tomato sauce on the bread, put a slice of low-fat cheese on the sauce; top with fresh tomato, olives, green pepper. Bake in the oven or toaster oven. Top off the meal with a favorite fruit cup and a serving of nuts.

- Make a sandwich with either sliced turkey, tuna, or veggie burger and add lettuce, tomato and low fat mayo or mustard. Top off the meal with a favorite fruit cup and a serving of nuts.

Nutritious, Easy to Prepare Breakfasts

- A bowl of whole grain or vitamin fortified cereal (e.g., Cheerios, Total) or oatmeal with fruit (banana, strawberries, peaches) and either low fat milk or soy / rice milk. Plus a glass of orange juice.

- Toast two slices of whole grain bread (wheat, pumpernickel, raisin, etc). with non-hydrogenated peanut butter and a glass of orange juice. Add some figs or prunes if desired.

- Toast a bagel or English muffin (whole wheat if possible) and add non-hydrogenated peanut butter or a slice of low fat cheese. Add a glass of orange juice and some figs or prunes if desired.

Chapter # 51: How to Reduce Your Level of Anxiety

What are some symptoms of anxiety? (You don't have to experience all of these symptoms to be anxious)

- Worry or Obsessional thinking

- Muscle Tension (back, neck, jaw)

- Heart Pounding

- Trembling

- Shortness of breath

- Chest Pain

- Nausea

- Stomach Problems

- Dizziness

- Lightheadedness

- Feelings of Unreality (Spaced Out)

- Fear of Losing Control

- Chills

- Hot Flashes

- Restlessness

- Compulsive Hair Pulling

- Compulsive or Ritualistic Behaviors (e.g., hand washing)

Common reasons for feeling anxious.

- Feeling that you have little or no control over what happens in your life.

- Being fearful or worrying about the unknown (e.g., doing something you've never done before, visiting a place you've never been to, meeting someone for the first time, etc.).

- Concern for how others will judge you or potentially reject you (e.g., your boss, an audience, a date, etc.).

- Feeling overly attached to another person (e.g., parent, spouse, girl/boyfriend) and anticipating separation from this person.

- Repercussions of a traumatic event (e.g., natural disaster, rape, abuse, etc.).

- Exposure to a specific stimulus (e.g., animals, heights, flying, etc.) that is, a phobia.

How to reduce your level of anxiety.

- Regular **exercise** (See Chapter # 33).

- Daily **relaxation** (See Chapter # 38).

- Reduce your intake of caffeine (i.e., coffee, sodas).

- **Distract** (See Chapter # 44) yourself (Lose yourself in an interesting activity, Listen to relaxing **music** (See Chapter # 08), etc.)

- **Expressing** (See Chapter # 42) the nature of your anxiety:

    1. To a caring, nonjudgmental, person who is a good listener
    2. To a mental health professional
    3. In a **non-verbal** (See Chapter # 06) way

- Try to pinpoint the origin of your anxiety (e.g., a specific situation, person, or event).

- **Stimulus Control** (See Chapter # 13) - Avoid those situations which make you anxious (if you can).

- Stop **worrying** (See Chapter # 52) - change your thinking; evaluate if your fears or expectations are feasible or likely?

- **Thought Stopping** - When experiencing unwanted or intrusive thoughts, picture a large STOP sign in your mind and yell (out loud or to yourself) STOP!!

- Get **organized** (See Chapter # 39).

- **Problem Solving** (See Chapter # 40) - Make important decisions which may be unresolved.

- **Gain control** - anything you can do (i.e., to change your thinking or behaviors) which gives you a sense of control should lessen your anxiety somewhat.

- **Behavioral rehearsal** (See Chapter # 15) (e.g., before giving a public speech).

- **Systematic Exposure** (See Chapter # 17) (slowly, step-by-step, exposing yourself to feared situations) - ideal for phobias.

- **Spiritual** (See Chapter # 29) methods (e.g., prayer).

"Success is not the key to happiness. Happiness is the key to success. If you love what you are doing, you will be successful."

Albert Schweitzer

Chapter # 52: Stop Worrying

It is difficult (if not impossible) to worry and be happy at the same time. Therefore, to be happier, you must worry less. How does one worry less, you may ask. Try the following tips:

■ Determine if there is anything constructive you can do to deal with the problem or situation you are worrying about. If possible, take action and plan how to **eliminate the problem** (See Chapter # 40). There is nothing wrong with thinking about important issues in your life; looking at a situation from many angles, or asking others about their opinions. Worry, though, is pointless rumination. Nothing is accomplished by it other than making you feel worse. It is helpful to ask yourself, "Is there anything I can do about *X* right now?" If there is, take action or plan when you will take action. Otherwise, distract yourself (see below).

■ If you have determined that there is nothing you can do right now to deal with the situation you are worrying about, **distract** (See Chapter # 44) yourself. For example, watch T.V., read a book, exercise. You can talk to someone about what's worrying you if that diminishes your worrying. If it does not, or makes it worse, talk about other topics not related to your worrisome situation.

■ Remember, most situations that we worry about never come true. In fact, research indicates that 90% of what we worry about never comes true. To prove this to yourself, write down a list of your worries and keep track of how many actually come to pass.

■ Finally, there are unforeseen things that can happen (accidents, natural disasters, etc.). Other than taking basic safety precautions, there is nothing you can do to prevent them. If you are preoccupied with what bad things could happen, you are robbing yourself of the quality time you could be experiencing right now.

"Whoever is happy will make others happy, too."

Mark Twain

Chapter # 53: How to Become Less Depressed

Note: If you are suffering from clinical depression, please see a mental health professional. The following suggestions may be used in conjunction with professional treatment.

What are some symptoms of depression? (You don't have to experience all of these symptoms to be depressed)

- Sadness or Depressed Mood

- Loss of Interest, Pleasure, or Motivation

- Weight Loss or Gain

- Insomnia (Sleeping too little), Hypersomnia (Sleeping too much)

- Fatigue, Restlessness

- Feelings of Worthlessness

- Decreased Ability to Concentrate

- Suicidal Ideation (Seek immediate professional help if you are suicidal)

Common reasons for feeling depressed.

- Feeling "stuck" in a situation where you believe there is no escape and/or no choices.

- Feeling angry either at yourself and/or others and internalizing this anger rather than expressing it.

- Experiencing numerous and/or lengthy stressful life events (traumas, losses, etc.).

How to reduce your level of depression.

- Try to pinpoint the origin of your depression (e.g., a specific situation, person, or event). Sometimes just knowing what is causing your depression may be helpful.

- Review what Life Stressors you may be experiencing (See Chapter # 04).

- Are your Basic Human Needs being fulfilled? (See Chapter # 03).

- Are you using Negative Coping Styles to ease your depression or are these styles promoting your depression? (See Chapter # 05).

- Depression is often associated with fatigue and lack of motivation. Therefore, anything you can do to "re-activate" is helpful. (For example, see below).

  1. Regular **exercise** (See Chapter # 33).

  2. Review Ways to Help Motivate Yourself. (Make complex tasks more manageable by breaking them down, one step at a time) (See Chapters # 47-48).

  3. Try to engage in Leisure Activities, Hobbies, Etc. (See Chapter # 32).

- **Expressing** (See Chapter # 42) the nature of your depression to a caring, nonjudgmental, person who is a good listener, or a mental health professional (or expressing yourself in non-verbal ways).

- If you have unresolved problems, try **Problem Solving** (See Chapter # 40) - Make important decisions which may be unresolved.

- To combat feelings of worthlessness and/or negativity:

  1. Catch negative, self-defeating thoughts as they occur, and reframe them into more **positive** (See Chapter # 28) thoughts.

  2. Raise your **self-esteem** (See Chapter # 58).

  3. Review A List of **Positive Statements** to Repeat to Yourself Everyday (See Chapter # 31).

- To combat impaired **sleep** See Chapter # 54.

- If you have unexpressed **anger** See Chapter # 49.

- If your feelings of depression surround **interpersonal** (See Chapter # 18-21) relationships, change the nature of your relationships by choosing who you deal with, and how you deal with people.

- If your depressed feelings occur exclusively during winter months, you may want to **Use Light to Improve Your Mood** (See Chapter # 09).

- Sometimes you may have to **Accept Certain Unchangeable Situations** (See Chapter # 23).

Chapter # 54: Importance Of, Ways to Promote Quality Sleep

Why do we sleep?

There is no definitive answer to this question, but sleep probably helps us replenish both our physical and emotional energy. The number of hours of sleep that people need varies from person to person and may tend to decrease as one ages. The average is 8 hours (with a range of 4 to 10 hours).

What happens when we don't sleep well?

We may feel tired, irritable, depressed or mentally dull. Our performance on many tasks is impaired (speaking, writing, reaction time, problem-solving, learning, and memory). If you only lose an hour or two of sleep occasionally, the above mentioned problems will probably not occur. Chronic sleep deprivation could cause such problems though.

What causes sleep problems?

Sleep disturbance may be caused by a variety of physical, emotional, or behavioral problems.

- Physical Problems

    1. Waking up to urinate - older individuals usually awaken in the middle of the night to urinate. If this late-night awakening is disturbing to you, you may want to drink less several hours before going to bed (you should drink more during the day to avoid dehydration).

    2. Drinking Alcohol - although it could initially help you get to sleep, as it wears off you may wake up. Alcohol disturbs the normal sleep cycle and should be avoided several hours before going to bed.

    3. Taking stimulants - stimulants like caffeine are in coffee, chocolate, cocoa and tea. They can keep you awake if taken too close to bedtime. People have different sensitivities to caffeine. You may want to experiment to see how much of it affects you before bedtime (i.e., drink less or drink earlier in the day to see if it affects your sleep).

    4. Pain - If you experience pain which interferes with your sleep, you may need to consult a physician to treat the pain.

- Emotional Problems

  1. If you are experiencing stressful events in your life, it may temporarily disturb your sleep until the situation is resolved.

  2. Worrying or thinking about things before going to bed can make it difficult to fall asleep.

  3. Nightmares can wake you up and can be very distressing.

  4. Those individuals suffering from Clinical Depression may either want to sleep all the time or awaken early in the morning (at least one hour before their normal wake-up time) with difficulty getting back to sleep.

- Behavioral Problems

  1. Jet lag disturbs the normal sleep cycle.

  2. Working a rotating or night shift is difficult to adjust to for some people. Individuals may chronically get too little sleep.

  3. Sleeping on an uncomfortable mattress.

  4. Temperature - some people have difficulty sleeping when it is too hot.

  5. A snoring bed partner (This is not your behavior, but the behavior of your partner which interferes with sleep).

What is insomnia?

When you felt like you haven't slept long enough or the sleep was not refreshing. You may have trouble falling asleep, wake up in the middle of the night and can't get back to sleep, or wake up too early in the morning.

How to treat sleep problems.

If you are experiencing frequent sleep difficulties, you may want to consult a physician and/or try some of the following suggestions. There is no one single remedy that works for everyone. You may have to try several strategies until you find one or several that work for you. Also, it may take several weeks to establish a new sleep pattern. There are some basics of "Sleep Hygiene" which can be helpful. These include:

- Have a regular bedtime and sleep schedule. Go to bed at the same time and wake up at the same time everyday.

- Try to do relaxing or mindless activities before going to bed. Anything that stimulates you (e.g., a book that you can't put down, discussing important life issues, etc.) may get your mind thinking and prevent you from falling asleep.

- Avoid caffeine (soda, coffee, chocolate) for the period between lunch and sleep.

- Do regular aerobic **exercise** (See Chapter # 33) in the late afternoon to early evening (at least 3 hours before bedtime). Don't exercise too close to bedtime as this may stimulate you.

- If possible, avoid naps during the day. If you do nap, avoid napping after 2 p.m. and allow yourself at most one half-hour nap a day.

- Go to bed and if you can't fall asleep within 20 minutes, get out of bed and do something that you find relaxing. Avoid trying too hard to get to sleep.

- If you worry while lying in bed (many people worry at night since this may be the only time they are not busy or occupied with things to do) you can try two techniques:

  1. Write these thoughts/worries down on paper as a way to get them "out of your mind"; you can then go back over them at another time.

  2. **Distract** (See Chapter # 44) yourself from the thoughts. The main thing to remember is to keep your attention on a task and avoid thoughts of everything else. You can use a variety of techniques like:

- **Relaxation** methods (See Chapter # 38)

  ▸ Tense-and-release muscles
  ▸ Breathing - either try regular breaths or count the breaths
  ▸ Imagery - Picture yourself in a relaxing place (sights, sounds, touch; e.g., the beach)

- **Counting**

  ▸ Yes, the old cliche about counting sheep can work
  ▸ Count backwards from 245 or any other high number

- If you suffer from frequent nightmares you may want to talk to someone about them or write them down. **Expression** (See Chapter # 42) of the feelings/events surrounding the dreams may help alleviate them.

- Put alarm clocks out of site (A time-free environment is helpful to falling asleep).

- Take a hot bath 2-4 hours before going to bed (leads to cooling of the body around midnight resulting in better sleeping).

- Try warm milk or a light snack before bed (hunger can disrupt sleep) but avoid rich foods.

- Assess if any nighttime noises are waking you up (snoring, barking, etc.).

- Make sure you are getting the Recommend Daily Allotment of Magnesium (magnesium-rich foods include bananas, nuts, beans, leafy greens, and wheat germ). A deficiency in magnesium can inhibit quality sleep.

- Sex (more so for men than women) can relax you and help you to fall asleep.

- Sleep on a comfortable mattress.

- If possible avoid sleep medications. These medications can change your REM cycle, become addictive, or make getting to sleep without them even more difficult. If you use them, please do so only occasionally.

- Melatonin - The research on this hormone is equivocal. Some studies indicate that it works while other do not. There are some potentially troublesome side effects as well. Product purity is unknown since it is not regulated by the FDA.

- If you are experiencing early morning awakening and feel depressed, you may want to consider psychological/psychiatric treatment for depression.

- Stop smoking. Nicotine stimulates brain-wave activity and increases blood pressure and heart rate. These factors all disturb your ability to get to sleep and remain asleep.

- Make sure you have a dark sleep environment.

- Check the effect of the medications you are taking on sleep.

- Increase exposure to bright light and natural light during the day and early evening.

"The best way to cheer yourself up is to try to cheer somebody else up."
Mark Twain

Chapter # 55: How to Age More Slowly and Gracefully

Everyone gets older and eventually dies. There's no way (yet) to avoid this process of decline and death. But, we can delay and improve the aging process by changing our habits. It's never too late to start, but of course, the younger we start, the better. If you perform the following behaviors, you will look and feel younger for longer.

1. **Eat** right (See Chapter # 50). (And eat less; Research indicates that both rodents and primates live longer when they eat reduced calorie diets that are nutritionally balanced.

2. Don't smoke.

3. Drink in moderation or not at all.

4. Maintain a **positive** (See Chapter # 28) mental attitude.

5. Reduce your exposure to the sun to prevent wrinkles and skin cancer.

6. **Exercise** (See Chapter # 33) - The following is a partial list of the benefits of exercise which are particularly relevant to aging individuals. (SEE YOUR PHYSICIAN BEFORE BEGINNING ANY EXERCISE PROGRAM).

- Gives you more energy and vigor to meet the demands of your daily life, and provides you with a reserve to meet the demands of unexpected emergencies.

- Helps improve short-term memory in older individuals.

- Improves your mental alertness.

- Improves mental cognition - a short-term effect only.

- Keeps your weight down so you appear in better physical shape.

- Reduces your risk of having a stroke.

- Improves the functioning of the body's immune system.

- Improves overall physical health.

- Helps to relieve constipation.

- Provides you with protection from injury.

- May extend life span.

- Reduces risk of heart attack/heart disease.

- Improves your body posture.

- Increases your level of muscle strength.

- Helps to retard bone loss as you age, thereby reducing your risk of developing osteoporosis.

- Increases the density and breaking strength of your ligaments and tendons.

- Increases the thickness of the cartilage in your joints.

- Slows the rate of joint degeneration if you suffer from osteoarthritis.

- Improves your pain tolerance and mood, if you suffer from osteoarthritis.

- Maintains or improves your level of joint flexibility.

- Improves balance and coordination.

- Helps you to maintain an independent lifestyle.

- Enhances sexual desire, performance and satisfaction.

- Eases the discomfort of arthritis.

- Physically active elderly people perform better than sedentary elderly people on cognitive tasks such as reasoning, vocabulary, memory and reaction time (Robert Dustman, Ph.D. Veterans Administration, Salt Lake City)

Chapter # 56: How to Boost Your Immune System

By engaging in the following behaviors, you can probably boost your immune system. (**WARNING:** If you are ill or frequently get sick, do not hesitate to seek medical attention; These suggestions are not intended as a substitute for medical advise from a physician; please see your physician before beginning any new exercise program.).

1. Increase the number and quality of your **social relationships** (See Chapter # 18-21).

2. Get enough **exercise** (See Chapter # 33).

3. Reduce your level of stress and **relax** (See Chapter # 38).

4. **Laugh** more (See Chapter # 41) .

5. Be more **optimistic** (See Chapter # 28) (i.e., have a positive outlook on life).

"There is only one happiness in life,
to love and be loved."

George Sand

Chapter # 57: Behavioral Ways To Help Lower Your Blood Pressure

For some individuals, changing your behaviors can help lower your blood pressure. (**WARNING:** These suggestions are not intended as a substitute for medical advise from a physician; Please see your physician before beginning any new exercise program, and if you have high blood pressure follow his/her advice).

The following are a list of things you can do to lower blood pressure:

1. Reduce your level of stress by eliminating stressors or coping with them better.

2. **Eat** a proper diet. (See Chapter # 50). (Especially, by lowering your salt intake.

3. Get enough **exercise** (See Chapter # 33).

4. **Pet** a dog, cat, etc. (See Chapter # 35).

5. Increase quality **social contacts** (See Chapter # 18) with others.

"When one door of happiness closes, another opens; but often we look so long at the closed door that we do not see the one which has been opened for us."

Helen Keller

Chapter # 58: Raising Your Self-Esteem

Having high self-esteem can be broken down into four personal qualities:

1. **Liking yourself** - In order to be truly happy, you must feel good about yourself most of the time. There are many reasons to like yourself:

   - Just because you are a living, human being
   - All of your good qualities (make a list of them)
   - The **meaningful** (See Chapter # 46) and worthwhile things you will do or have done
   - The **goals** (See Chapter # 47) you will accomplish or have accomplished

2. **Accepting yourself** - A large part of having high self-esteem is accepting yourself for all your shortcomings, inadequacies, and bad points. Happy people have just as many shortcomings as unhappy people. The difference is that happy people accept their shortcomings as natural, human, and acceptable; and they like themselves anyway. Unhappy people make themselves miserable, put themselves down, and criticize themselves for the very same shortcomings. Nobody's perfect, and happy people don't expect to be. They accept both their strengths and weaknesses as parts of a total, well-rounded human being. So it pays to stop being perfectionistic and making yourself suffer for natural inadequacies that all people have. It's all a matter of choice: Accept it or make yourself miserable about it - the choice is yours.

3. **Knowing yourself** - "Knowing yourself" means knowing:

   - Your short and long-term goals and how you plan to achieve them.

   - What your **needs** are (See Chapter # 03), and how you plan to get them fulfilled.

   - Your own particular pattern of behaviors and how they affect others.

   - Your own particular identity (who you are), as defined by:

     ▸ Your *own* beliefs and values, not those of your family, friends, culture, etc.
     ▸ Your role (mother, father, husband, wife, brother, sister, son, daughter)
     ▸ Religion (Christian, Jew, etc.)
     ▸ Nationality (American, Mexican, etc.)
     ▸ Job (plumber, housewife, engineer, etc.)
     ▸ Family background (e.g., I'm a 4th generation McCoy originally

from Ireland, etc.)

4. **Being yourself** - It is important to live your own life and not live just to please others. Try not to be overly concerned about what others think of you. While everyone likes approval from others, it may not be worth compromising your beliefs to gain such approval. Not everyone will like you, even if you try to please them all of the time. Being yourself makes you feel free; it will make you much prouder of yourself, and it will attract to you the kind of people who are *right* for you (those who like you just the way you are).

Chapter # 59: How to Get, Deal With, and Enjoy Your Job

Job satisfaction is important to our happiness. Work can give us a sense of identity, mastery, meaning, and purpose. It rewards us both emotionally and financially. It can provide us with a sense of belonging or pride. Ideally, it is best to work as a way to enjoy life, not just for money. If you really enjoy what you do, the money will probably follow. If you hate your job, try to leave it. If you can't or won't, find some part of the job that you can enjoy. People tend to be more satisfied doing meaningful work rather than having endless periods of leisure time or idleness. In fact, unemployment is associated with declining mental and physical health in most people.

SUGGESTIONS FOR IMPROVING JOB ENJOYMENT

- Job satisfaction usually increases where workers have more control in making decisions (e.g., hours, job goals, etc.) rather than someone else making all the decisions.

- The relationship between salary and job satisfaction is complex; studies seem to indicate that satisfaction is related more to the perception that one is being paid fairly, rather than to the actual amount of money received.

- To maximize job satisfaction, don't become overwhelmed with too many things to do (stress) or underwhelmed with too few things to do (boredom).

- Ideally, one should pursue a job where you can become fully engrossed in what you do; where your skills are fully engaged; where there is challenge, and variety; where you feel you are making a difference, and you are doing something that you feel will have an impact.

- You will enjoy your job more if it has personal significance and meaning.

FINDING THE RIGHT JOB FOR YOU:

Here are some questions to ask yourself:

- What do I find meaningful and significant and how can I apply those priorities towards my career choice.

- What are my interests (hobbies, activities, etc. Write a list of them.) Can I find a career which incorporates some of my interests?

- How much education am I willing to pursue beyond high school (consider time, expense, lost wages)? Do I want to go to college, graduate school or perhaps a vocational school?

- What are my abilities (book smarts, persuasive talker, etc.)?

- Do I like working with my hands or my head, or both?

- Do I like working with others or mostly by myself?

ADVISE TO THE JOB SEEKER:

- Volunteer at a job you think you might like.

- Take a class in a job area you are interested in to see if you like it.

- Talk to a person who is doing the job you are interested in and ask him/her questions.

- Investigate whether there is a demand for the job you are interested in pursuing.

- Seek vocational counseling at a local college or state employment office.

WHERE TO FIND A JOB:

Your public library or the Internet can provide you with information on:

- Career planning
- Detailed descriptions of hundreds of job types
- Industries
- Prospective employers
- Financial aid
- Relocation to new cities
- Writing a Resume
- Job listings

HERE ARE SOME JOB SEARCH TECHNIQUES:

- Ask friends, family, etc. if they know of any job openings
- Answering advertisements in local/out-of-town newspapers
- Placing personal advertisements (work wanted)
- Going to federal, state employment agencies
- Calling job hotlines
- Looking at job listings at the chamber of commerce, local government,

hospitals, and other major employers
- Volunteering in community projects or special events which may lead to permanent employment
- Calling a temp agency
- Visiting in-person a business (e.g., retail store) and filling out an application
- Calling businesses to see if they have any openings (use Telephone Directory)
- Employment Agency
- Mailing a resume directly to a company
- Contacting executive recruiting/search firms
- Contacting your college placement office
- Join a job club
- Join a professional organization and "network"
- The Internet

DEALING WITH JOB STRESS

To diminish job stress, there are on-the-job and off-the-job factors to consider:

- ON-THE-JOB

  - **Manage your time** (See Chapter # 39) effectively (become organized, prioritize duties from most to least important, delegate responsibilities rather than trying to do it all).

  - Learn how to deal with **others** (See Chapters # 18-22) effectively and use coping skills as needed.

- OFF-THE-JOB

Don't forget to:

- **Exercise** (See Chapter # 33)

- **Relax** (See Chapter # 38)

- **Sleep** (See Chapter # 54) well.

This should reduce your overall level of stress.

"The true way to render ourselves happy is to love our work and find in it our pleasure."

Francoise de Motteville

Chapter # 60: Money Can Provide a Source of Pleasure and/or Stress. Can it Buy Happiness?

1. Well, yes and no. Yes, in that money can buy the essentials (food, clothing, shelter, etc.) and these essentials are necessary for happiness. If you don't have enough of these necessities, you will not be very happy. In other words, a person who does not have enough money to buy the basics will, most likely, be less happy than a person who does. However, someone who has vastly more money (i.e., rich) is not necessarily any happier than someone with just the basics. This may be surprising, but many surveys of wealthy and middle class people indicate that rich people are no happier than those people with modest incomes.

2. Of course, money can give people more freedom and control to do what they want to do with their lives. Nevertheless, rich or poor, people need **meaningful activities** (See Chapter # 46). If you have a lot of money and no meaningful endeavors other than acquiring material goods, you will feel unfulfilled.

3. If you feel that you need to be rich to be happy: You will spend a lot of time trying to acquire wealth and may be ignoring those endeavors which *will* bring you happiness (time with family and friends, meaningful pursuits, etc.). Conversely, if you lower your monetary expectations (i.e., have fewer wants) a great weight can be lifted off your shoulders. You don't have to be a celebrity, world famous, or fabulously wealthy to be happy. It is within reach. In fact, there is accumulating evidence that striving for power, fame, wealth, and material goods--big parts of the "American Dream"--more than for good relationships, personal growth, and altruism is associated with more anxiety, more depression, and poorer general functioning (Kasser & Ryan, 1993).

"Happiness is not in the mere possession of money; it lies in the joy of achievement, in the thrill of creative effort."

Franklin D. Roosevelt

Chapter # 61: How to Save Money and Ease Financial Problems

Financial problems are a source of stress for many people. Here are some suggestions to get your financial house in order and save money (Note: the following are not a substitute for legal or financial advice from a professional):

<u>General Advice</u>

1. Try to eat out at restaurants as little as possible. Eating out can be quite expensive.

2. Try to avoid buying on impulse. Ask yourself do I really need this thing? Will I use it often or will it end up in the closet?

3. In general, it pays to shop around. Comparison shopping will enable you to find the lowest price around. If you can call stores by phone rather than driving there in-person, do so; it will save time and gasoline. Also using the Internet is a great way to comparison shop.

4. Use coupons.

5. Buy things on sale.

6. Subscribe to Consumer Reports Magazine or look for it in your local library. It will help to get information about a product or service that you are interested in; learn about unbiased evaluations of product quality; and help you get a reliable product that you will enjoy.

7. Ask about potential group discounts (American Automobile Assn., Senior Citizen, Veteran, Student, Group or Association, etc.) It doesn't hurt to ask.

8. Consider asking a salesperson if this is the lowest price available for something you want to buy. The salesperson may be able to tell you about an upcoming sale or beat the price of a competitor.

9. Consider buying in bulk. Warehouse Clubs like Sams, Costco, or BJ's can save you money if you shop there often enough to justify the yearly membership fee ($40-$55).

TRANSPORTATION

Airline Fares

1.   You can lower the price of a round-trip air fare by as much as two thirds by making certain your trip includes a Saturday evening stay over, and by purchasing the ticket in advance.

2.   To make certain you have a cheap fare, even if you use a travel agent, call all the airlines that fly where you want to go and ask what the lowest fare to your destination is. Or compare prices using the Internet.

3.   Keep an eye out for "fare wars." Be prepared to act quickly.

Car Rental

1.   Since car rental rates can vary greatly, shop around for the best basic rates and special offers.

2.   Rental car companies offer various insurance and waiver options. Check with your insurance agent and credit card company in advance to avoid duplicating any coverage you may already have.

New Cars

1.   You can save thousands of dollars over the lifetime of a car by selecting a reliable car that requires fewer repairs (See Consumer Reports Magazine for objective comparisons).

2.   Consider paying cash for your car instead of financing or leasing. It will save you thousands of dollars in finance charges.

3.   Consider buying a fuel efficient car instead of a "gas guzzler."

4.   Having selected a model, you can save hundreds of dollars by comparison shopping. Use the Internet or Consumer Reports Magazine to find out what the "Invoice price" of the car is (or what the dealer paid for the car). Call at least five dealers for price quotes and let each know that you are calling others. When negotiating the price, don't discuss trade-ins until you have finalized the price of the car; then you can discuss a trade-in (Although you will get more money selling a car privately than trading it in).

Used Cars

1. Before buying any used car:

   ■ Compare the seller's asking price with the average retail price in a "bluebook" or other guide to car prices found at many libraries, banks, credit unions and the internet.

   ■ Have a mechanic you trust check the car, especially if the car is sold "as is."

2. Consider purchasing a used car from an individual you know and trust. They are more likely than other sellers to charge a lower price and point out any problems with the car.

Auto Leasing

1. Don't decide to lease a car just because the payments are lower than a traditional auto loan. The leasing payments may be lower because you don't own the car at the end of the lease.

2. Leasing a car is very complicated. When shopping, consider the price of the car (known as the capitalized cost), your trade-in allowance, any down payment, monthly payments, various fees (excess mileage, excess "wear and tear," end-of-lease), and the cost of buying the car at the end of the lease.

Gasoline

1. You can save hundreds of dollars a year by using the lowest octane called for in your owner's manual.

2. You can save up to $100 a year on gas by keeping your engine tuned and your tires inflated to their proper pressure.

3. Purchase a fuel efficient car.

Car Repairs

Consumers lose billions of dollars each year on unneeded or poorly done car repairs. The most important step that you can take to save money on these repairs is to find a skilled, honest mechanic. Before you need repairs, look for a mechanic who:

■ is certified and well established;
■ has done good work for someone you know; and

- communicates well about repair options and costs.

INSURANCE

Auto Insurance

1. You can save several hundred dollars a year by purchasing auto insurance from a licensed, low-price insurer. Call your state insurance department for a publication showing typical prices charged by different companies. Then call at least four of the lowest-priced, licensed insurers to learn what they would charge you for the same coverage.

2. Talk to your agent or insurer about raising your deductibles on collision and comprehensive coverage's to at least $500 or, if you have an old car, dropping these coverage's altogether. Taking these steps can save you hundreds of dollars a year.

3. Make certain that your new policy is in effect before dropping your old one.

Homeowner Insurance

1. You can save $100 or more a year by purchasing homeowner insurance from a low-price, licensed insurer. Ask your state insurance department for a publication showing typical prices charged by different licensed companies. Then call at least four of the lowest priced insurers to learn what they would charge you. If such a publication is not available, it is even more important to call at least four insurers for price quotes.

2. Make certain you purchase enough coverage to replace the house and its contents.

3. Make certain your new policy is in effect before dropping your old one.

Life Insurance

1. If you want insurance protection only, buy a term life insurance policy.

2. If you want to buy a whole life, universal life, or other cash value policy, plan to hold it for at least 15 years. Canceling these policies after only a few years can more than double your life insurance costs.

3. Check your public library for information about the financial soundness of insurance companies and the prices they charge.

BANKING/CREDIT

Checking

1. You can save more than $100 a year in fees by selecting a checking account with a minimum balance requirement that you can, and do, meet.

2. Banking institutions often will drop or lower checking fees if paychecks are directly deposited by your employer. Direct deposit offers the additional advantages of convenience, security, and immediate access to your money.

Savings and Investment Products

1. Before opening a savings or investment account with a bank or other financial institution, find out whether the account is insured by the federal government. An increasing number of products offered by these institutions, including mutual stock funds and annuities, are not insured.

2. To earn the highest return on savings (annual percentage yield) with little or no risk, consider certificates of deposit (CDs) and treasury bills or notes.

3. Once you select a type of savings or investment product, compare rates offered by different institutions. These rates can vary a lot and, over time, can significantly affect interest earnings.

Credit Cards

1. You can save as much as several hundred dollars each year in lower credit card interest charges by paying off your entire bill each month.

2. If you are unable to pay off a large balance, switch to a credit card with a low annual percentage rate (APR).

3. You can reduce credit card fees, which may add up to more than $100 a year, by getting rid of all but one or two cards, by avoiding late payment and over-the-credit limit fees, or using credit cards with no annual fee.

Auto Loans

1. Consider making a large down payment or even paying for the car in cash. This could save you as much as several thousand dollars in finance charges.

2. You can save as much as hundreds of dollars in finance charges by shopping for the cheapest loan. Contact several banks, your credit union, and the auto manufacturer's own finance company.

First Mortgage Loans

1. You may save tens of thousands of dollars in interest charges by shopping for the shortest-term mortgage you can afford. On a $100,000 fixed-rate loan at 8% annual percentage rate (APR), for example, you will pay $90,000 less in interest on a 15-year mortgage than on a 30-year mortgage.

2. You can save thousands of dollars in interest charges by shopping for the lowest-rate mortgage with the fewest points. On a 15-year, $100,000 fixed-rate mortgage, just lowering the APR from 8.5% to 8.0% can save you more than $5,000 in interest charges. On this mortgage, paying two points instead of three would save you an additional $1,000.

3. If your local newspaper does not periodically run mortgage rate surveys, call at least six lenders for information about their rates (APRs), points, and fees. Then ask an accountant to compute precisely how much each mortgage option will cost and its tax implications.

4. Be aware that the interest rate on most adjustable rate mortgage loans (ARMs) can vary a great deal over the lifetime of the mortgage. An increase of several percentage points might raise payments by hundreds of dollars per month.

Mortgage Refinancing

Consider refinancing your mortgage if you can get a rate that is at least one percentage point lower than your existing mortgage rate and plan to keep the new mortgage for several years or more. Ask an accountant to calculate precisely how much your new mortgage (including up front fees) will cost and whether, in the long run, it will cost less than your current mortgage.

<u>Home Equity Loans</u>

1. Be cautious in taking out home equity loans. These loans reduce the equity that you have built up in your home. If you are unable to make payments, you could lose your home.

2. Compare home equity loans offered by at least four banking institutions. In comparing these loans, consider not only the annual percentage rate (APR) but also points, closing costs, other fees, and the index for any variable rate changes.

HOUSING

<u>Home Purchase</u>

1. You can often negotiate a lower sale price by employing a buyer broker who works for you, not the seller. If the buyer broker or the broker's firm also lists properties, there may be a conflict of interest, so ask them to tell you if they are showing you a property that they have listed.

2. Do not purchase any house until it has been examined by a home inspector that you selected.

<u>Renting a Place to Live</u>

1. Do not limit your rental housing search to classified ads or referrals from friends and acquaintances. Select buildings where you would like to live and contact their building manager or owner to see if anything is available.

2. Remember that signing a lease probably obligates you to make all monthly payments for the term of the agreement.

<u>Home Improvement</u>

1. Home repairs often cost thousands of dollars and are the subject of frequent complaints. Select from among several well established, licensed contractors who have submitted written, fixed-price bids for the work.

2. Do not sign any contract that requires full payment before satisfactory completion of the work.

Major Appliances

1. Consult Consumer Reports, available in most public libraries, for information about specific brands and how to evaluate them, including energy use. There are often great price and quality differences among brands.

2. Once you've selected a brand, compare stores on the internet or check the phone book to learn what stores carry this brand; then call at least four of these stores for the prices of specific models. After each store has given you a quote, ask if that's the lowest price they can offer you. This comparison shopping can save you as much as $100 or more.

UTILITIES

Electricity

1. To save as much as hundreds of dollars a year on electricity, make certain that any new appliances you purchase, especially air conditioners and furnaces, are energy-efficient. Information on the energy efficiency of major appliances is found on Energy Guide Labels required by federal law. Check with your electric utility to learn if it has a program to help reduce the costs of any appliance purchases.

2. Enrolling in load management programs and off-hour rate programs offered by your electric utility may save you up to $100 a year in electricity costs. Call your electric utility for information about these cost-saving programs.

Home Heating

A home energy audit can identify ways to save up to hundreds of dollars a year on home heating (and air conditioning). Ask your electric or gas utility if they can do this audit for free or for a reasonable charge. If they cannot, ask them to refer you to a qualified professional.

Local Telephone Service

1. Check with your phone company to see whether a flat rate or measured service plan will save you the most money.

2. Check your local phone bill to see if you have optional services that you don't really need or use. Each option you drop could save

you $40 or more each year.

Long Distance Telephone Service

1. If you make more than a few long distance calls each month, consider subscribing to a calling plan. Call several long distance companies to see which one has the least expensive plan for the calls you make. Surprisingly, many people don't have any idea what they pay per minute on their long distance calls. Don't subscribe to a plan with a high monthly fee unless you make a lot of long distance calls.

2. Whenever possible, dial your long distance calls directly. Using the operator to complete a call can cost you an extra $1 to $3.

3. If you have unlimited night or weekend calling on your cellphone plan, make your long distance calls during these times.

Food Purchased at Markets

1. You can save hundreds of dollars a year by shopping at the lower-priced food stores. Convenience stores often charge the highest prices.

2. You will spend less on food if you shop with a list.

3. You can save hundreds of dollars a year by comparing price- per-ounce or other unit prices on shelf labels. Stock up on those items with low per-unit costs.

Prescription Drugs

1. Since brand name drugs are usually much more expensive than their generic equivalents, ask your physician and pharmacist for generic drugs whenever appropriate.

2. Since pharmacies may charge widely different prices for the same medicine, call several. When taking a drug for a long time, also consider calling mail-order pharmacies, which often charge lower prices.

Funeral Arrangements

1. Make your wishes known about your funeral, memorial, or burial arrangements in writing. Be cautious about prepaying because there may be risks involved.

2. For information about the least costly options, which could save you several thousand dollars, contact a local memorial society, which is usually listed in the Yellow Pages under funeral services.

3. Before selecting a funeral home, call several and ask for prices of specific goods and services, or visit them to obtain an itemized price list. You are entitled to this information by law and, by using it to comparison shop, you can save hundreds of dollars.

Chapter # 62: When Distraction Gets Out of Control

■ Some people use distraction to an extreme. They compulsively try to keep busy and/or distract themselves using **negative coping styles** (See Chapter # 05).

■ They may use distraction as a way to avoid important issues that they would rather not deal with. Distraction may be effective in the short term, but if important issues are being avoided, further problems may occur in the long term.

■ It may be appropriate to "deal" with these issues in an appropriate environment like therapy or self-help (See **problem-solving** (Chapter # 40) or **expression of thoughts and feelings** (Chapter # 42)) for appropriate self-help information).

"Before we set our hearts too much on anything, let us examine how happy are those who already possess it."

François Duc de La Rochefoucauld

Epilogue

Now that you have read through all these suggestions, remember that happiness is for the most part a choice. If you get just <u>one</u> helpful hint that makes your life a little happier, then this book has accomplished its goal. I believe that by getting your needs met and dealing with life in a positive way, you have a very good chance for a healthy, happy and productive life.

Appendices

Appendix # 1- 2Steps2Happiness Action Plan

2Steps2Happiness Action Plan		
Start Date:	**Step**	**Motivators (see below for numbers**
	I will reduce or stop the following Negative Coping Style(s):	
	I will fulfill the following Human Needs which are not being met:	
	I will decide which life stressors can be *eliminated* or *reduced* and do so (e.g., change jobs, end bad relationships):	
	I will begin using the following Positive Coping Styles:	

Motivator # 1
Break goals down into small steps. Make slow, steady progress and give yourself rewards when you accomplish a small step. If you can't carry out a small step, break it down even further and try an even smaller step. Be persistent. Keep trying until you achieve these steps and don't worry if you stumble, experience setbacks, or make mistakes along the way. This is normal and should be expected. It may be helpful to write down each step in detail. Remember, make sure your goal is realistic and achievable.

Motivator # 2
Write down all the positive things you will achieve by accomplishing this goal and keep them handy. Look at them often to remind yourself of all the benefits you can have. Write down all the reasons you don't want to continue doing things the way you have always done them.

Motivator # 3
Write down reasons that you may be resistant to achieving this goal (e.g., others may treat me differently, fear of the unknown, fear of rejection, etc.). Try to counteract these negative thoughts with more positive and, perhaps, realistic thoughts.

Motivator # 4
Try accomplishing your goals with others. For example, exercising with a friend can help you stay motivated to keep exercising. You can encourage each other to persevere. Also, the social interaction will make the process of achieving your goal more enjoyable.

Appendix # 2 - Positive Coping Techniques

Positive Coping Techniques

Indicate which Positive Coping Techniques you will <u>not</u> use, you will try using in the <u>future</u>, or that you <u>already</u> use to fulfill your needs and/or cope with stressors

Positive Coping Techniques	Not Interested	I'm going to try to do this more	I already do this enough
Express your thoughts and feelings **verbally** to a caring, nonjudgmental person			
Express your thoughts and feelings through **writing** (e.g., a journal)			
Express your thoughts and feelings through **Artistic Expression** (e.g., poetry, painting, sculpture, music)			
Express your thoughts and feelings through **movement** of your body (e.g., dance, yoga, martial arts)			
Pretend to be happy by **moving the muscles of your face** into a smile			
Listen to **music** as a way to relax or become stimulated			
Increase or decrease available **lighting** to relax or become stimulated			
View beautiful **nature scenes** (water, plants, sky, mountains)			
Change **colors** in your environment as a way to relax or become stimulated			
Adjust **air** temperature, humidity, and flow to improve mood			
Get a **massage** to relax			
Get **wet** (shower, hot bath, sauna, a swim) to improve mood			
Smell pleasant scents to improve mood (e.g., floral)			
Eat a balanced diet			

Positive Coping Techniques	Not Interested	I'm going to try to do this more	I already do this enough
Drink enough water			
Remove things from your life that are "bad" for you (e.g., stay away from smokers if you're trying to quit smoking) and/or include "good" things that promote positive behaviors (e.g., exercise better when listening to music) (**Stimulus Control**)			
Model or imitate behaviors of people you respect			
Practice new behaviors until they become easier for you to do (e.g., learn public speaking) (**Behavioral rehearsal or role-playing**)			
Reward yourself and others for positive behaviors you wish to encourage			
Slowly, step-by-step, **expose** yourself to feared situations until they become less scary (**Systematic Exposure**)			
Use appropriate **body language** when speaking with others (eye contact, etc.)			
Listen well to others			
Compromise with others rather than always having to get your way			
Show **genuine interest** in others			
Express **appreciation** towards others for their efforts and actions			
Use **humor** and don't take yourself too seriously			
Display good **manners** towards others (respectful, considerate, polite)			
Give others positive as well as negative **feedback**			

Positive Coping Techniques	Not Interested	I'm going to try to do this more	I already do this enough
Don't expect **perfection** from yourself or others			
Don't try to **change** other people			
Apologize if you make a mistake			
Be aware of, understand, and appreciate the feelings of others (**Empathy**)			
Defend your rights and openly express your thoughts, beliefs, and feelings in a direct, nondestructive fashion			
Say **No** when necessary			
Ask for favors when necessary			
Initiate, continue, and **terminate** conversations with others			
End relationships with others when necessary			
Differentiate between the things in life you have control over and those you don't; **Accept** the things you cannot change, and change the things you can			
Compare yourself to those people less fortunate than you			
Enjoy the **present** and **savor** life's little pleasures			
Count your **Blessings** (make a list)			
Have **Realistic Expectations** of yourself and others			
Be more **optimistic** (look on the bright side of events, i.e., the silver lining)			
Utilize **Spirituality** as a way to feel better about your life			

Positive Coping Techniques	Not Interested	I'm going to try to do this more	I already do this enough
Repeat positive statements to yourself (**Self Affirmations**)			
Try new enjoyable Leisure **Activities**, Hobbies, Etc.			
Engage in regular **Exercise**			
Enjoy the company of a **Pet**			
Volunteer your time			
Perform "**Deep Breathing**" Relaxation Exercises			
Perform "**Tense and Release**" Muscle Relaxation Exercises			
Perform "**Heavy Feet**" Relaxation Exercises			
Perform "**Hand Warming**" Relaxation Exercises			
Perform "**Imagery**" Relaxation Exercises			
Perform "**Meditation**" Relaxation Exercises			
Use "**Problem Solving**" when trying to make a decision			
Seek out opportunities to **laugh** (e.g., funny people, books)			
Use **Distraction** to divert your thoughts from worry or pain			
Make complex tasks more manageable by **breaking them down**, one step at a time			
Write down the rewards you will achieve by engaging in new or scary behaviors			
Get enough **sleep**			

Positive Coping Techniques	Not Interested	I'm going to try to do this more	I already do this enough
Spend money wisely (don't try to buy happiness with things; reduce debt and financial problems by spending less)			
Be **responsible** (do what you say you are going to do) or let other's know when you cannot fulfill your promise			
Reduce your intake of **caffeine** (soda, coffee)			
Establish **meaningful goals** and make a plan to accomplish them			

Activities/Hobbies		
ACTIVITIES YOU CURRENTLY ENJOY	**ACTIVITIES YOU'VE DONE IN THE PAST, BUT DON'T DO**	**ACTIVITIES YOU WOULD LIKE TO TRY IN THE FUTURE**

Appendix # 4 - Weight Loss Action Plan

Weight Loss Action Plan		
Name:		
Current Weight:_____	Goal Weight: _____	
Type of Exercise and Frequency:	❏ Treadmill ❏ Stationary Bike ❏ Walking ❏ Running ❏ Swimming ❏ Tennis ❏ Cycling ❏ Hiking ❏ Weight-lifting ❏ Organized sports (hockey, soft-ball, etc.) ❏ Other _____	<u>Initial</u> __ Minutes per day __ times per week <u>Target</u> __ Minutes per day __ times per week
Self-Rewards for Completed Goals (e.g., buy new clothes, music cd, etc.)	1 2 3 4	
List of Activities to Substitute For Eating	❏ Listen To Music ❏ Exercise ❏ Talk to Someone ❏ Perform a Hobby ❏ Chew Gum ❏ Relaxation Exercises ❏ Take a bath ❏ Play with your pet	Other: ❏ _____ ❏ _____ ❏ _____ ❏ _____
Positive Coping Techniques (See Appendix # 2)	Refer to as Needed	
Grocery Shopping List (See Appendix # 5)	Refer to when Grocery Shopping	

Write Meals on Calendar (See Appendix # 6)	Write down Daily	
Weigh self and measure waistline once per week (See Appendix # 6)	Refer to Weekly	
List of Potential Snack Foods	❏ Chewing gum ❏ Trail-Mix Bars ❏ Air-Popped Popcorn ❏ Pretzels (hard) ❏ Jell-O ❏ Dried Fruits (e.g., Figs, Prunes) ❏ Nuts (Almonds, Walnuts, pistachios) ❏ Cereals like Cheerios, Puffed rice or wheat ❏ Dark Chocolate ❏ Non-sugared beverages	Other: ❏ _____ ❏ _____ ❏ _____ ❏ _____ ❏ _____
Current Frequency of Eating Out at Restaurants: ___ times per week	Desired Frequency of Eating Out at Restaurants: ___ times per week	

Identify Triggers for Emotional Eating, Compulsive Eating, or Overeating	❏ Social situations ❏ Watching Television ❏ Food in plain sight ❏ _____ ❏ _____ ❏ _____ ❏ _____ ❏ _____	Emotional Reasons ❏ Comfort yourself ❏ Numb emotional pain ❏ Cope with stress ❏ Cope with depression ❏ Cope with boredom ❏ Cope with anger ❏ Cope with emptiness ❏ Cope with loneliness ❏ Feeling helpless ❏ Fearfulness ❏ Feelings of inadequacy
Potentially Problematic Situations and solutions (e.g., going to a fast food restaurant with others)	Situation	Solution

Appendix # 5 - Grocery Shopping List

Grocery Shopping List	
<ul><li>Remember, if you don't want to eat it, <u>Don't Buy It</u>!</li><li>Read the labels as you shop and pay attention to serving size and servings per container.</li><li>When comparing items, try to choose foods that are lower in sodium, saturated fat and transfat.</li></ul>	
Food Category	**Examples**
Baked Products	Whole Grain products like Bagels, Bread, Matzo, Pancakes, Raisin Bread, Tortillas, Pita Bread, Crackers
Beverages	Water, Seltzer, Postum, Tea, Orange Juice, Soy Milk, Low Sodium V8, Pineapple Juice, Rice Milk, 100% real fruit juice without added sugar
Cereals and Grains	Oatmeal, Toasted Oats, Total, Wheat Germ, Weetabix, Kashi, Brown Rice, Shredded Wheat, Puffed Wheat, Pasta, Popcorn
Dairy and Egg Products	Smart Balance; Cheese: Those with five grams of saturated fat or less per ounce like Swiss Cheese, Parmesan Cheese, Mozzarella Cheese, Ricotta (Part Skim Milk); Eggs (Not Fried), Low Fat Plain Yogurt, Skim Milk
Fats and Oils	Olive Oil, Canola Oil (Compare amount of Saturated Fat)
Fish	Tuna, Salmon, Gefilte Fish, Sardines, Imitation Crab Meat and Other Fresh Fish
Fruits	Apples, Dried Apricots, Avocados, Bananas, Blueberries, Cherries, Dates, Figs, Fruit Cocktail, Grapes, Grapefruit, Mangos, Melons, Nectarines, Olives, Oranges, Peaches, Pears, Pineapple, Plums, Prunes, Raisins, Strawberries, Tangerines, Watermelon, etc.
Legumes	Beans, Chickpeas, Lentils, Peanuts, Peas, Soy Beans, Non-Hydrogenated Peanut Butter (Smucker's Natural Peanut Butter)
Prepared Food	Healthy Choice Meals, Veggie Burgers, Soy Products (Soy burgers, Soy hot dogs, Soy deli slices, Soy ground round etc.) (check labels)
Nuts and Seeds	Almonds, Walnuts, Pistachio Nuts, Sunflower Seeds (Pick ones with lowest amount of Saturated Fat)
Poultry Products	Chicken Breast, Turkey Breast (Preferably white meat without the skin)

Snacks and Sweets	Chewing gum, Trail-Mix Bars, Air-Popped Popcorn, Pretzels (hard, whole-wheat), Jell-O, Dried Fruits, Cereals like Cheerios or Total, Puffed Rice, Small Amounts of Dark Chocolate
Soups, Sauces, and Gravies	Salsa, Tomato based Spaghetti Sauce, Teriyaki, Minestrone Soup, Pea Soup, Vegetarian Vegetable Soup, other low sodium soups (e.g., Healthy Choice or Campbell's Healthy Request Soups), Ketchup
Spices and Herbs	Vinegar, Mustard, Low Fat Mayo or Canola-based Mayo; Garlic, Curry Powder, Parsley, Oregano, Pepper, etc.
Vegetables	Asparagus, Arugula, Avocado, Beet greens, Bok choy, Broccoli, Brussels sprouts, Cabbage, Carrots, Celery, Collard Greens, Corn, Frozen Mixed Vegetables, Kale, Peas, Potatoes, Romaine Lettuce, Rutabaga, Spinach, Swiss or red chard, Tomatoes, Turnips, Turnip Greens, and Watercress. etc.
Beef and Pork	Lean Cuts like Round, Sirloin/loin, Flank, Tenderloin, Ground Round, Ham

Appendix # 6 - Food/Weight Tracking Charts

Sunday	Monday	Tuesday	Wednesday	Thursday	Friday	Saturday

	Weight	Waist Size
Week 1		
Week 2		
Week 3		
Week 4		
Week 5		
Week 6		
Week 7		
Week 8		
Week 9		
Week 10		
Week 11		
Week 12		

Appendix # 7 - Refrigerator Reminder Page

Refrigerator Reminder Page (Place This Page on Your Refrigerator As a Constant Reminder)	6. Self-Rewards for Completed Goals:

Keeping Motivated

1. I will maintain a healthy weight and I will maintain a positive attitude even if I slip up occasionally.

2. I care about my health and will act accordingly

3. Benefits of Weight Loss
   - Better Health
   - Lower Health Care Costs
   - Positive Feedback from Others
   - Gain Energy and Agility
   - Increased Self-Worth
   - Look Better
   - Live Longer

4. Potential Negative Health Consequences Of Being Overweight
   - Hypertension
   - Abnormal levels of blood lipids
   - Type 2 diabetes
   - Coronary Heart Disease
   - Stroke
   - Gallbladder Disease
   - Osteoarthritis
   - Sleep Apnea
   - Respiratory Problems
   - Gout
   - Endometrial, Breast, Prostate, and Colon Cancers

5. Emotional and Moral Support From People (Face-to-Face, Phone, Online) List People Below:

_____

_____

6. Self-Rewards for Completed Goals:

_____

_____

_____

7. List of Activities to Substitute For Eating
   - Listen To Music
   - Exercise
   - Talk to Someone
   - Perform a Hobby
   - Chew Gum
   - Relaxation Exercises
   - Other Pleasurable Activities (bath, play with your pet, etc.)

8. Snacks

If during the evening while watching television you get the "munchies," eat low-calorie nutritious snacks like air popped popcorn, puffed wheat or rice, cereal, celery, or fruit. You could also have a small portion of nuts.

Place Unflattering Picture Below:

Appendix # 8 - Food Substitution Chart

Substitute This.....	*With This...*
Potato Chips	Pretzels, Almonds, Toasted Oats (Cheerios), Puffed Wheat or Rice
Fried Foods	Baked, Roasted, Steamed, Poached, Broiled Foods (or occasionally Grilled)
Sugared Sodas, Alcoholic Beverages	Water, Seltzer, Fruit Juices like Orange Juice (Watch the Sugar content), Low Sodium V8 or Tomato Juice, Tea, Artificial Sweetener Sucralose (Splenda)
Donuts	Bagels
White Rice	Brown Rice, Kashi, Lentils, Chickpeas, Pasta
Sugared Cereals	Low-sugar cereals and / or Whole grains (Oatmeal, Cheerios, Wheat germ, Puffed Wheat, All Bran, Total)
White Bread	Wheat Bread or Dark Breads without transfats
Hamburgers	Soy Burgers, Veggie Burgers, Ground Turkey
Red Meat	Turkey, Chicken, Fish, Eggs, Tofu
Hash Browns	Oatmeal, Baked Potatoes
Hydrogenated Peanut Butter	Non Hydrogenated Peanut Butter (e.g., Smuckers Natural Peanut Butter)
Snacks (candy bars, cake, cookies, etc.)	Dried Fruit, Fresh Fruit, Trail Mix Bars, Popcorn, Puffed Rice or Wheat, Carrots, Celery, Nuts, Whole Grain Cereals, Roasted Soy Nuts, Other Sliced Vegetables
Regular Milk	Low Fat Milk (1 or 2%), Soy or Rice Milk
Sour Cream	Low Fat or No Fat Yogurt or Cottage Cheese
Butter	I Can't Believe It's Not Butter, Smart Beat, Take Control Spread, etc.

Substitute This.....	With This...
Mayonnaise (Regular)	Mustard, Salsa, Mayo (Low Fat) or Canola Oil Mayo
Salt	**Herbs** (basil, bay leaf, garlic, oregano, rosemary, thyme) **Spices** (cinnamon, ginger, cumin, nutmeg) and **Seasonings** (chili powder, curry powder), Lemon or Lime
Cream Cheese	Mozzarella, Ricotta, Low Fat Swiss, Soy Cheese
French Fries, Tater Tots	Baked Potato, Beans, Pasta, Rice
Cream or Beef Soups	Low Sodium Soups like Chicken Soup, Vegetable Soup, Bean Soup, Lentil Soup
Deli Meats (e.g., Bologna, Pastrami, Corned Beef)	Freshly prepared meats (Chicken, Turkey) or canned fish (like Tuna, Salmon, or Sardines)
Bacon, Sausage, Hot Dogs, Salami	Roast Beef, Turkey, Soy Hot Dogs
Ice Cream	Sherbet, Italian Ices, Yogurt
Cream Sauces	Tomato based sauces
High Saturated Fat Salad Dressings	Dressings low in Saturated Fat like Olive Oil, Canola Oil Salad Dressings or Honey Mustard, Balsamic Vinegar, etc.
Saturated Fats (cream, butter, lard, palm oil, coconut oil)	Unsaturated Fats (e.g., olive oil, sunflower seed oil, peanut oil, fish oil, avocado, olives, walnuts, almonds)

Appendix # 9 - Serving Sizes

HOW MANY SERVINGS DO YOU NEED EACH DAY?			
Food Group	Children ages 2 to 6 years, women, some older adults (about 1,600 calories)	Older children, teen girls, active women, most men (about 2,200 calories)	Teen boys, active men (about 2,800 calories)
Bread, Cereal, Rice, and Pasta Group (Grains Group) - especially whole grain	6	9	11
Vegetable Group	3	4	5
Fruit Group	2	3	4
Milk, Yogurt, and Cheese Group (Milk Group) - preferably fat free or low fat	2 or 3	2 or 3	2 or 3
Meat, Poultry, Fish, Dry Beans, Eggs, and Nuts Group (Meat and Beans Group) - preferably lean or low fat	2, for a total of 5 ounces	2, for a total of 6 ounces	3, for a total of 7 ounces

WHAT COUNTS AS A SERVING?	
Bread, Cereal, Rice and Pasta Group (Grains Group) - whole grain and refined 1 slice of bread; About 1 cup of ready-to-eat cereal; ½ cup of cooked cereal, rice, or pasta	**Milk, Yogurt, and Cheese Group (Milk Group)** 1 cup of milk or yogurt; 1 ½ ounces of natural cheese (such as Cheddar); 2 ounces of processed cheese (such as American)
Vegetable Group 1 cup of raw leafy vegetables; ½ cup of other vegetables - cooked or raw; 3/4 cup of vegetable juice	**Meat, Poultry, Fish, Dry Beans, Eggs, and Nuts Group (Meat and Beans Group)** 2-3 ounces of cooked lean meat, poultry, or fish; ½ cup of cooked dry beans or ½ cup of tofu counts as 1 ounce of lean meat; 2 ½ ounce soyburger or 1 egg counts as 1 ounce of lean meat; 2 tablespoons of peanut butter or 1/3 cup of nuts counts as 1 ounce of meat
Fruit Group 1 medium apple, banana, orange, pear; ½ cup of chopped, cooked or canned fruit; 3/4 cup of fruit juice	

Appendix # 10 - RDA/Read a Label Charts

RDA = Required Daily Allowance (USDA approved); SA = Safe and Adequate Allowance

Overall Nutrients				Vitamins			
Calories	2000.0	_cal	100%	Vit. A	5000.0	_IU	100% RDA
Protein	55.000	_gm	100% RDA	Vit. B6	1.600	_mg	100% RDA
Total Fat	65.000	_gm	100%	Vit. B12	2.000	_mcg	100% RDA
Sat. Fat	20.000	_gm	100%	Vit. C	60.000	_mg	100% RDA
Mono. Fat	28.889	_gm	100%	Vit. E	8.000	_mg	100% RDA
Poly. Fat	6.667	_gm	100%	Thiamine	1.100	_mg	100% RDA
Carbo.	300.00	_gm	100%	Folacin	180.00	_mcg	100% RDA
Fiber	30.000	_gm	100%	Riboflavin	1.300	_mg	100% RDA
Cholesterol	300.00	_mg	100%	Niacin	15.000	_mg	100% RDA
				Panto. Acid	5.000	_mg	100% SA
Minerals							
Calcium	1200.0	_mg	100% RDA	Phosphorus	1200.0	_mg	100% RDA
Copper	2.000	_mg	100% SA	Potassium	2000.0	_mg	100% RDA
Iron	15.000	_mg	100% RDA	Selenium	55.000	_mcg	100% RDA
Magnesium	280.00	_mg	100% RDA	Sodium	2400.0	_mg	100% SA
Manganese	3.000	_mg	100% SA	Zinc	12.000	_mg	100% RDA

HOW TO READ A NUTRITION FACTS LABEL

Macaroni & Cheese

Nutrition Facts

Start Here → Serving Size 1 cup (228g)
Servings Per Container 2

Amount Per Serving

Calories 250   Calories from Fat 110

% Daily Value*

Limit these Nutrients:
Total Fat 12g — 18%
  Saturated Fat 3g — 15%
Cholesterol 30mg — 10%
Sodium 470mg — 20%
Total Carbohydrate 31g — 10%
  Dietary Fiber 0g — 0%
  Sugars 5g
Protein 5g

Get Enough of these Nutrients:
Vitamin A — 4%
Vitamin C — 2%
Calcium — 20%
Iron — 4%

*Percent Daily Values are based on a 2,000 calorie diet. Your Daily Values may be higher or lower depending on your calorie needs:

	Calories:	2,000	2,500
Total Fat	Less than	65g	80g
Sat Fat	Less than	20g	25g
Cholesterol	Less than	300mg	300mg
Sodium	Less than	2,400mg	2,400mg
Total Carbohydrate		300g	375g
Dietary Fiber		25g	30g

Quick Guide To % Daily Value
5% or Less is Low
20% or More is High